# Oneness

# Oneness

## GREAT PRINCIPLES SHARED
## BY ALL RELIGIONS

*Jeffrey Moses*

BALLANTINE BOOKS • NEW YORK

Library of Congress Control Number: 2002094156

ISBN 0-345-45763-3

Text design by Kris Tobiassen
Cover design by Monica Benalcazar
Cover photo © Michael Townsend/Getty Images

Manufactured in the United States of America

First Revised and Expanded Edition: November 2002

1   3   5   7   9   10   8   6   4   2

# CONTENTS

# ONENESS

Throughout the ages, the scriptures of all religions have proclaimed that humanity is one great family. This is a simple truth, and it is simply and directly stated in every religion. In fact, almost all the principles that are associated with religious thought are shared by every religion. The Golden Rule, Love Thy Neighbor, Honor Thy Father and Mother, Speak Truth, It Is More Blessed to Give Than to Receive—these precepts and many others are common to all religions, and are very similarly expressed in each.

When their inherent similarities are revealed, the collected wisdom of the world's religions shows a profound "Oneness" of the human spirit. When placed side by side—with surprisingly similar wording in many instances—the essential beliefs shared by all religions confirm that our differences are superficial, and that our similarities are deep.

They have the overwhelming effect of creating unity, where differences dissolve and the soul can wonder, Why do we have such conflicts?

These volumes of spiritual wisdom have another value, on a very personal level for each individual. When their most fundamental themes are gathered and compared directly, as in this book, they become like a guide or a blueprint for the inner development of mind and spirit. They form the basis not only for how nations can live together peacefully, but also for how individuals can structure their lives to achieve success, happiness, and spiritual fulfillment.

This book is the result of research that took place over many years. There are numerous volumes of scriptures for many of the world's religions, each with varying translations, the majority in archaic and complex language. Yet as I read through the scriptures, the universally familiar sayings jumped forth. Each, when discovered, was like a nugget that seemed to have been waiting for centuries to be uncovered and directly compared to similar expressions in other religions.

After several years of research, by 1981, I had gathered sayings for about twenty important and widely recognized main principles. At that time, it was unheard of to compare directly the line-by-line similarities of religious texts. I felt that I needed validation that my research was meaningful—and that it would encourage harmony, not further division.

It so happened that Mother Teresa, who had recently won the Nobel Peace Prize, was in the United States, visiting her missions around the country. Feeling that she, of all people, was admired by followers of many religions, I contacted her, showing her my collection of compared sayings. I had the opportunity to speak with her on several occasions. She greatly appreciated the concept of *Oneness*, and she was kind enough to write an introduction for the book.

With my resolve strengthened, I continued my research. Within a year I had compiled a self-published edition that included sayings for twenty-five central principles. Several bookstore managers I approached with the book were fascinated by the concept. One placed a thick stack of books in a stand by the cash register. Two days later he called asking for more copies.

He described what he had observed in customers' faces as they flipped through the pages and understood what the book was about. "Their eyes lit up—surprised to have suddenly found something they had been looking for in many places for a long time."

In 1989, the Ballantine Publishing Group published the first edition of *Oneness: Great Principles Shared by All Religions.* That edition, which had thirty central principles, included an introduction and special prayer by Mother Teresa, as well as a testimonial by the Dalai Lama, who was awarded the Nobel Peace Prize a few months after *Oneness* was released.

Since then I have continued my research, expanding to sixty-four the number of great central principles that appear in this current book.

In every scripture, the great principles are repeated and re-phrased in various ways. To keep the book simple and read-able, however, I have chosen one representative saying from each religion.

As an example, the principle Honor Thy Father and Mother is universal to all religions. The following sayings are all found in the scriptures of Islam. Only the first saying was used in *Oneness*, but the others are just as beautiful and appropriate.

Serve and revere your parents. Heaven is spread beneath the feet of mothers everywhere.

*Hadith*

He who wants to enter Paradise at the best door must please his father and mother.

*Hadith*

Thy Lord hath decreed that ye worship none but Him, and that ye be kind to parents. Whether one or both of them attain old age in thy life, say not to them a word of contempt, nor repel them, but address them in terms of honor.

*Qur'an 17:23*

There is no child who is a doer of good to his parents who God will not look at with great favor.

*Hadith*

We have enjoined on man (to be good) to his parents: in travail upon travail did his mother bear him, and in years twain was his weaning.

*Qur'an 31:14*

"Messenger of God, who is most deserving of friendly care from me?" Mohammed replied, "Your mother." He asked who came next, and He replied, "Your mother." He asked who came next and He replied, "Your mother." He asked who came next and He replied, "Your father."

*Hadith*

Similarly, numerous expressions of Honor Thy Father and Mother (and for all the other principles contained in *Oneness*) could have been cited from Christianity, Judaism, Buddhism, and from all other religions. To do so, however, would have sacrificed the readability of the book. *Oneness* includes a simple collection of sayings written on facing pages in an uncluttered way. My hope is that the silence of the white page surrounding the quotes gives the reader's soul a chance to assimilate the comparisons, and to contemplate the great truths contained in each.

I encourage anyone who is interested to read from the scriptures directly. For information about how to locate the scriptures, please refer to the section Sources and Suggested Readings near the end of this book.

Since the time of writing and publishing the first *Oneness*, the world has changed tremendously. Tragic events continue to unsettle our hopes for achieving lasting peace and harmony. At these times, when emotional tensions threaten the inherent spirituality of life, it is natural to turn toward the divine teachings to strengthen and renew us. Their unshatterable unity has the power to bring humankind to a new level of understanding that restores peace, dignity, and respect for others.

Many people today seek their own laws. Yet, in so doing, they often find only partial values of these universal principles. Others of us, seeking to restore feelings of comfort and security, are more committed than ever to uncovering the fundamental shared values of all religions. The full values of these timeless concepts have been recorded similarly in all major religions since time immemorial. The principles of inner development are no different now than they were in the days of Jesus, Buddha, Mohammed, Moses, or Confucius. These great masters offer similar messages that have not become less essential for people in the modern world. These principles extend beyond time and change. They establish a clearly marked path that will enable each individual to attain the peace and enlightenment that is the ultimate goal in life.

— JEFFREY MOSES

# INTRODUCTION
## by His Holiness the Dalai Lama

All the world's major religions have a similar aim, so harmony between them is both important and necessary. I firmly believe that although they may have substantial differences of philosophical outlook, all religions have the same potential to be of help to mankind. Each emphasizes methods for improving human beings by developing such qualities as generosity, love, compassion, and respect for others.

All sentient beings want happiness and try to avoid suffering. This common experience is reflected in the common themes of love and compassion found in all religions. The apparent philosophical differences are similarly a reflection of people's different interests and inclinations. To make such differences a cause for conflict would be in contradiction to the broader religious aim of establishing peace and harmony. A comparison of sayings from the different religious traditions, such as the ones in this book, will certainly engender a deeper awareness of the qualities they have in common. This in turn will contribute to a greater sense of harmony and respect between them.

# Oneness

Oneness

# The Golden Rule

The Golden Rule is the cornerstone of religious understanding. It is the most complete expression of the Oneness of all people, serving as the foundation for peace and universal goodwill on earth.

The Golden Rule is expressed almost word for word in every religion. So fundamental is it to all religious thought that the founders and enlightened teachers of every religion have commented on it directly.

Jesus referred to the Golden Rule as "the law and the prophets." Mohammed described it as "the noblest expression of religion." Rabbi Hillel stated in the Jewish Talmud that the Golden Rule is "the whole of the Torah and the remainder is but commentary." Vyasa, the enlightened Hindu sage, called it "the sum of all true righteousness." Similarly, Buddha referred to it as "the sum total of all righteousness." And Confucius, the great Chinese master, deemed it "the one principle upon which one's whole life may proceed."

Many people are taught from childhood that living the Golden Rule is an ideal, without emphasizing the practical benefits. When people look upon others as extensions of themselves, all obstacles to fulfillment are removed—both for individuals and society. When the goals of every individual are supported by the activities of every other person, the world has the possibility to flourish in peace and prosperity. For this reason, the Golden Rule should not be thought of as a vague ideal. It is a practical principle that embodies the deepest aspirations of humanity. It serves as the basis for all that is positive and lasting in human life.

# The Golden Rule

Do unto others as you would have them do unto you, for this is the law and the prophets.

*Christianity*

What is hurtful to yourself do not to your fellow man. That is the whole of the Torah and the remainder is but commentary.

*Judaism*

Do unto all men as you would they should unto you, and reject for others what you would reject for yourself.

*Islam*

Hurt not others with that which pains yourself.

*Buddhism*

# The Golden Rule

Tzu Kung asked: "Is there any one principle upon which one's whole life may proceed?" Confucius replied: "Is not Reciprocity such a principle?—what you do not yourself desire, do not put before others."

*Confucianism*

This is the sum of all true righteousness—
Treat others, as thou wouldst thyself be treated.
Do nothing to thy neighbor, which hereafter
Thou wouldst not have thy neighbor do to thee.

*Hinduism*

Treat others as thou wouldst be treated thyself.

*Sikhism*

A man should wander about treating all creatures as he himself would be treated.

*Jainism*

Regard your neighbor's gain as your own gain; and regard your neighbor's loss as your own loss, even as though you were in their place.

*Taoism*

Ascribe not to any soul that which thou wouldst not have ascribed to thee.

*Bahá'í*

# Love Thy Neighbor

In the Gospel of Luke, Jesus is asked, "Who is my neighbor?" This question is just as relevant to us today, in our world made small by modern travel and nearly instantaneous communication.

In reply to this question, Jesus relates the parable of the Good Samaritan, who goes out of his way to help an injured man, even though of a different faith. In this parable, Jesus states directly and simply that all people are our neighbors and are worthy of respect and assistance—whether members of our own religion or any other. Just so, in the Hadith sayings of Islam, Mohammed says, "Assist any person oppressed, whether Muslim or non-Muslim." And Vyasa declares in the Bhagavad Gita of Hinduism, "He whose love is alike to friend and foe . . . that man is dear to Me [God]."

Every human being is born with an innate love for others. As a person matures, this love is put to many tests. But by understanding the teachings of the world's great religions, one can find the faith needed for love to endure.

More than a passing glance at the scriptures is necessary to achieve this level of understanding. Acts of faith, prayer, and deep meditation provide us with the strength that allows love for others to become an abiding part of our lives, of our beings. When many of us attain this type of faith, the expression of love in the world will be as spontaneous and natural as love between mother and child.

# Love Thy Neighbor

Thou shalt love thy neighbor as thyself.

*Judaism*

A new commandment I give to you, That you love one another; even as I have loved you . . . By this all men will know that you are my disciples, if you have love for one another.

*Christianity*

A man obtains a proper rule of action by looking on his neighbor as himself.

*Hinduism*

Full of love for all things in the world, practicing virtue in order to benefit others, this man alone is happy.

*Buddhism*

Seek to be in harmony with all your neighbors; live in amity with your brethren.

*Confucianism*

No one is a believer until he loves for his neighbor, and for his brother, what he loves for himself.

*Islam*

# The World Is Our Family

"The world is my family," says the Mahā Upanishad, a Vedic scripture of Hinduism with an oral tradition dating back more than six thousand years. From that beginning, every religion has proclaimed that the true basis for human life is understanding, compassion, forgiveness, charity, and assistance in every way toward others.

This principle stands as the foundation upon which all religious thought is based. Since we are all children of God, this principle states, we are related in a very fundamental way. Why, then, should we harm one another?

Most of the great principles included in this book are offshoots of the understanding that we are all one great family, related not only by blood but by an unbreakable spiritual bond.

# The World Is Our Family

God hath made of one blood all nations of men.

*Christianity*

All are the sons and daughters of God, good people all,
Brothers and Sisters, since created by One Father. No rooted
difference is there between them.

*Hinduism*

Have we not all one father? hath not one God created us?
why do we deal treacherously every man against his brother?

*Judaism*

All creatures are the family of God; and he is the most
beloved of God who does most good to His family.

*Islam*

# The World Is Our Family

Do not forget that the world is one great family . . . Regard Heaven as your father, Earth as your mother, and all things as your brothers and sisters.

*Shintoism*

God is the Father, Earth the Mother. With all things and in all things, we are relatives.

*Sioux*
*Native American*

# There Is One God

God is worshipped by billions of people throughout the world as the Almighty Beneficent Being. God is seen as One, without a second, omniscient, all-powerful, all-loving, and all-forgiving.

Although every religion proclaims that there is one God, the followers of a particular faith may feel that their God is unique, and different from the God of other faiths. Even though different religions may appreciate various aspects of God, this cannot diminish the wholeness of the Divine—and should not be the source of divisions between us.

Instead, our universal belief that there is one God should strengthen our convictions that an ultimate existence pervades all boundaries of the universe, and that all people and all things are of one essence.

# There Is One God

There is one God and Father of all, who is above all, and through all, and in you all.

*Christianity*

The Lord is God in heaven above and on the earth beneath; there is no other.

*Judaism*

He is the one God hidden in all beings, all-pervading, the Self within all beings, watching over all worlds, dwelling in all beings, the witness, the perceiver.

*Hinduism*

There is but one God whose name is true. He is the creator, immortal, unborn, self-existent.

*Sikhism*

All this is God. God is all that is.

*Sufism*

He, in truth, hath throughout eternity been one in His Essence, one in His attributes, one in His works.

*Bahá'í*

# More Blessed to Give
# Than to Receive

The wise handling of money can be as spiritually enriching as prayer. People who are in touch with their inner selves, and who truly care for others, experience their hearts spontaneously overflowing with the desire to help the less fortunate.

The giving of money, time, support, and encouragement to worthy causes can never be detrimental to the giver. The laws of giving are structured so that acts of charity open an individual to an unbounded reservoir of riches. Everything worthwhile in life has been created as the result of love and concern for others. When individuals give lovingly to those in need, they establish the basis for peace and are recognized for it by every nation.

# More Blessed to Give
# Than to Receive

It is more blessed to give than to receive.

*Christianity*

The Wise Man doth not hoard. The more he giveth, the more he hath; the more he watereth, the more is he watered himself.

*Taoism*

In the minds of the generous, contentment is produced.

*Sikhism*

Those who give in charity have lent to Allah a goodly loan.

*Islam*

# More Blessed to Give
# Than to Receive

The giving of a gift is superior to the acceptance of a gift.

*Hinduism*

Blessed is he that considereth the poor: the Lord will deliver him in time of trouble.

*Judaism*

# Do Not Harm Anything

If the intrinsic essence of each religion were captured in a single short phrase, the words would emphasize the importance of not harming others.

"Act always with loving kindness," says Buddhism. "Absence of hurtfulness is the ideal," states Hinduism. "Non-injury is the highest religion," Jainism proclaims. "Love does no wrong to a neighbor," declares Christianity. "Let a person withhold from doing harm to others," Islam declares. "Fight with no weapon but the word of God; use no means but a pure faith," asserts the scriptures of Sikhism.

We must always remember that the feelings and hopes of others are the same as ours. And we should never forget that all religions—which convey humanity's highest thoughts and aspirations—view all people in the world as one great family, created by God.

# Do Not Harm Anything

Do not hurt others, do no one injury by thought or deed, utter no word to pain thy fellow creatures.

*Hinduism*

Hurt none by word or deed, be consistent in well-doing.

*Buddhism*

Be ye kind to one another, tenderhearted, forgiving one another, even as God for Christ's sake hath forgiven you.

*Christianity*

One should do no harm to any living being, neither by thoughts nor words nor acts.

*Jainism*

Show kindness and mercy each to his brother.

*Judaism*

There should be neither harm nor reciprocating of harm.

*Islam*

# Preserve the Earth

The world's scriptures were written long before the earth was burdened with the intense levels of pollution that we have today. Even so, each religion emphasizes the importance of preserving the indigenous resources and beauty of our planet.

Our very existence depends upon the normal, healthful interaction of many different levels of the natural world—ranging from the smallest microbes to the vastness of the seas and atmosphere. When nature is defiled, every person ultimately suffers. For this reason, every religion states that nature should be preserved and that we must be aware and responsible for our interactions with the earth.

Preserving the ecology may be a problem affecting society as a whole, but the solution must come on the level of individuals. Only when people understand the universality of their own inner nature can they live harmoniously with the rest of the natural world. This is the basis for care of our planet: the growing worldwide awareness that the inner self of every person touches universal Being, uniting every person and every thing on earth.

# Preserve the Earth

The earth which drinketh in the rain that cometh oft upon it, and bringeth forth herbs . . . receiveth blessing from God.

*Christianity*

Do not contaminate the water. Do not throw your waste or leftover food into rivers and lakes. In this way, you guard the lives of all living beings abiding therein.

*Buddhism*

There is no Muslim who planteth a tree, or soweth a field, and man, birds or beasts benefit from them, but it is charity for him.

*Islam*

# Preserve the Earth

Take only what you need and leave the land as you found it.

*Arapaho*
*Native American*

Care should always be taken of trees and forests because of the many healthful effects they have for mankind.

*Hinduism*

If the seasons of agriculture be not interfered with, the grain will be more than can be eaten. If close nets are not allowed to enter the pools and ponds, the fish and turtles will be more than can be consumed. If the axes enter the hill-forests only at the proper times, the wood will be more than can be used.

*Confucianism*

# Heaven Is Within

Life is structured so that its finest, most meaningful aspects are often hidden from outer exposure. The sweetness of an orange is hidden within a bitter skin. The seed of a tree, from which life will spring, is protected within a hard shell. And a person may walk the earth, not knowing that a vast depository of riches lies hidden deep within the ground beneath his feet.

From earliest childhood, our senses respond to outward sensations. Without guidance and understanding, we could spend a lifetime appreciating the world only in an outward direction. But the true riches of life lie within. Through appreciation of the wisdom of the past, through prayer, and most of all, through deep meditation, we can become one with the inner silence that is a part of God.

When that silence is reached, it begins to radiate throughout all of one's activities. When a large number of individuals radiate this inner silence, heaven will begin to be seen on earth.

# Heaven Is Within

The kingdom of God cometh not with observation: neither
shall they say, Lo here! or, lo there! for, behold, the kingdom
of God is within you.

*Christianity*


What the undeveloped man seeks is outside; what the
advanced man seeks is within himself.

*Confucianism*


If you think the Law is outside yourself, you are embracing
not the absolute Law but some inferior teaching.

*Buddhism*

If human beings knew their own inner secrets, they would never look elsewhere seeking for happiness and peace.

*Sufism*

God bides hidden in the hearts of all.

*Hinduism*

God is in thy heart, yet thou searchest for Him in the wilderness.

*Sikhism*

# As Ye Sow, So Shall Ye Reap

All actions have far-reaching ramifications. "Unfathomable is the course of action," says the Bhagavad Gita, the most-beloved Hindu scripture. Because of this, we should be aware at all times that everything we do eventually could have an effect upon ourselves and our loved ones.

For those who are aware that this basic truth is the determining factor in achieving happiness and success, the hours of the day become an exercise in acting toward others with kindness and rightness.

The same is true for religions, cultures, and nations throughout the world. Those who want to live in peace must give peace to those who would war against them. Those who want respect for their own traditions must show respect for the traditions of others. Those who desire security must give security to those who do not have it.

These are fundamental laws of human life that cannot be violated. To act otherwise is to disregard the advice of the wisest people throughout history. Aware or unaware, all are ruled by this inevitable law of nature.

# As Ye Sow, So Shall Ye Reap

It is nature's rule, that as we sow, we shall reap.

*Buddhism*

Whatever a man sows, that he will also reap.

*Christianity*

As a man soweth so shall he reap.

*Sikhism*

A liberal man will be enriched, and one who waters will himself be watered.

*Judaism*

# As Ye Sow, So Shall Ye Reap

What proceeds from you will return to you.

*Confucianism*

Thou canst not gather what thou dost not sow; as thou dost plant the tree, so it will grow.

*Hinduism*

# Conquer with Love

In today's world, it is vital to understand that disagreements and conflicts between people or nations cannot be resolved through force. All religions are in complete agreement on this. Conquering others with force merely imprisons them. It does not remove the reasons underlying the conflict. Rather, it increases the tension and inevitably gives rise to even greater animosity.

Love, in contrast, is a unifying force. It radiates outward to resolve differences. It is not that the differences dissolve and are lost, but that they are integrated into a greater whole in which they are made more useful and beautiful.

Love conquers *before* there is fighting. Even if channels of communication have broken down and fighting breaks out, the underlying attitude should still be one of love and unification by love.

# Conquer with Love

Repay evil with good and, lo, he between whom and you there was enmity will become your warm friend.

*Islam*

Be not overcome of evil, but overcome evil with good.

*Christianity*

When one injures another, the injured turns around and injures the injurer. Similarly, when one cherishes another, the other cherishes the cherisher. One should frame one's rule of conduct according to this.

*Hinduism*

A soft answer turns away wrath, but a harsh word stirs up anger.

*Judaism*

Conquer your foe by force, and you increase his anger. Conquer by love, and you will reap no after sorrow.

*Buddhism*

Force, no matter how concealed, begets resistance.

*Lakota*
*Native American*

# Blessed Are the Peacemakers

Peace has been universally sought by all people in all times. It has been the goal of all law, religion, and politics. "Seek peace, and pursue it," proclaimed the Old Testament of the Holy Bible. "Have peace one with another," spoke Jesus in the Gospel of Mark. "If thine enemy incline towards peace, do you likewise incline towards peace," states the Holy Qur'an.

When people live in the awareness that there is a close kinship between all individuals and nations, peace is a natural result. Peace can come only as a result of concern and understanding for others. It can never be brought about by superficial negotiation or temporary agreement to end conflict.

Signatures on pieces of paper cannot bring harmony. Since the beginning of recorded history, tens of thousands of peace treaties have been signed. Clearly, treaties cannot sustain lasting peace. How could they? National borders, which are often created and supposedly protected by treaty, are artificial boundaries that ultimately create division among humankind. They do not promote the underlying feeling of unity that is vital in the creation of lasting peace.

Nor can the buildup of arms guarantee a nation's safety. This is a lesson that must be learned finally and absolutely. It is time now to look toward deeper, more lasting feelings of love and understanding between people. This and this alone can bring sustained harmony within the global community.

# Blessed Are the Peacemakers

Blessed are the peacemakers: for they shall be called the children of God.

*Christianity*

Shall I tell you what acts are better than fasting, charity, and prayers? Making peace between enemies are such acts; for enmity and malice tear up the heavenly rewards by the roots.

*Islam*

The noble minded dedicate themselves to the promotion of peace and happiness of others—even those who injure them.

*Hinduism*

To the counsellors of peace is joy.

*Judaism*

When a thought of war comes, oppose it by a stronger
thought of peace. A thought of hatred must be destroyed by
a more powerful thought of love.

*Bahá'í*

He heals divisions, and cements friendships; seeking peace,
and ensuring it, for in peace is his delight, and his words are
ever the words of a peacemaker.

*Buddhism*

# Truth Is Universal

The world's religions are like branches of the same tree. Each branch differs slightly from the others, but all are attached to the same trunk and draw nourishment from the same roots.

Taking this analogy further, it can be said that the roots represent the common source of all religions, the point of connection between human and Divine consciousness. Deep within each individual is an inner awareness that is part of the Universal awareness. The enlightened founders and teachers of every religion have drawn upon this source. Every religion was inspired by the Divine. The words of Jesus, Buddha, Mohammed, Moses, Shankara, and Confucius may vary—but their common message of the necessity for human compassion, understanding between people, and devotion to helping others deeply expresses the Oneness of the human spirit.

This message is unconquerable. Through the centuries, there have been certain governments, philosophic movements, and even religious sects that have promoted division among people for one reason or another. Time ultimately erases separation. Repeatedly truth has reawakened, and the intrinsic unity of all people has been realized.

A person can have no higher vocation than to assist the emergence of this understanding throughout the world. Those who become immersed in such activity find themselves inspired by God. They become guiding lights for the age arriving, when quarrels and differences will fade, and peace and harmony will come to the fore.

# Truth Is Universal

All scripture is inspired by God, and profitable for teaching, for reproof, for correction, and for training in righteousness, that the man of God may be complete, equipped for every good work.

*Christianity*

We believe in God, and that which hath been sent down to us, and that which hath been sent down to Abraham . . . and that which hath been given to Moses and to Jesus, and that which was given to the prophets from their Lord. We make no distinction between any of them: and to God are we resigned.

*Islam*

Do not decry other sects, do not deprecate others, but rather honor whatever in them is worthy of honor.

*Buddhism*

In varying ways the sages have described
The same unvarying and essential truths;
There is no real conflict between them all.

*Hinduism*

Truth does not depart from human nature. If what is
regarded as truth departs from human nature, it may not be
regarded as truth.

*Confucianism*

Allow us to recognize Thee in all Thy holy names and
forms: as Rama, as Krishna, as Shiva, as Buddha. Let us
know Thee as Abraham, as Solomon, as Zarathustra, as
Moses, as Jesus, as Mohammed, and in many other names
and forms, known and unknown to the world.

*Sufism*

# Better to Examine the Self

One of the central themes of every religion is the importance of understanding ourselves, and using that strength as the basis for all our activities. "Learn to know thyself," exclaims the Islamic faith. "If you know yourself well, your errors will be few," says Confucianism. "Knowledge of one's own self is stated to be the most excellent among all things, for it leads to enlightenment" states the Hindu religion.

Our activities and successes are based on our inner strength and wholeness. To grow, it is necessary for us to recognize and correct our own faults. Yet it is difficult to do this, since we often hide our shortcomings not only from others but also from ourselves.

When we gain the ability to recognize and correct our own bad habits, we begin to make rapid strides toward greater happiness and success in all spheres of life. Only by learning to admit to our own faults can we become more loving to others and more tolerant of their shortcomings.

# Better to Examine the Self

If you love others, and affection is not returned, look into your love. If you rule others, and they are unruly, look into your wisdom. If you treat others politely and they do not return your politeness, look into your respect. If your desires are not fulfilled by what you do, turn inward and examine yourself in every point.

*Confucianism*

First take the log out of your own eye, and then you will see clearly to take the speck out of your brother's eye.

*Christianity*

The ignorant observe others' faults, be they so little as a mustard seed. They overlook their own faults as large as bilva fruits.

*Hinduism*

# Better to Examine the Self

The faults of others we see easily; our own are very difficult to see. Our neighbor's faults we winnow eagerly, as chaff from grain; our own we hide away as a cheat hides a losing roll of the dice.

*Buddhism*

He who knows others is discerning; he who knows himself is wise.

*Taoism*

They who quarrel with others, instead of quarreling with their own hearts, waste their lives.

*Sikhism*

# Honor Thy Father and Mother

It would be difficult to repay our parents for the hours, days, and years they cared for us when we were young. Because of this, we honor them and care for them in their later years.

But why, in particular, does every religion place such overwhelming importance on the tradition of honoring parents? Perhaps because by doing so we support the entire fabric of society, sustaining our own well-being as well as that of our children, and our children's children.

From birth, the sustenance given by our parents is so essential and basic to life that in many religions and traditions, the universal qualities of God are expressed as personified archetypes of Father and Mother. These expressions seem natural and justified, and they remind us that the creative forces of the universe nourish and support us continually.

As expressed in the Native American tradition, "All living beings are from the earth. Wherever we look, we see part of our Mother and Father."

# Honor Thy Father and Mother

My son, keep your father's commandment, and forsake not your mother's teaching. Bind them upon your heart always; tie them about your neck. When you walk, they will lead you; when you lie down, they will watch over you; and when you awake, they will talk with you.

*Judaism*

For God commanded, saying, Honor thy father and mother.

*Christianity*

Honor thy Father and Mother. Forget not the favors thou hast received.

*Hinduism*

Serve and revere your parents. Heaven is spread beneath the feet of mothers everywhere.

*Islam*

To support Father and Mother,
To cherish Wife and Child,
To follow a peaceful calling,
This is the greatest blessing.

*Buddhism*

If each man would love his parents and show due respect to his elders, the whole empire would enjoy tranquillity.

*Confucianism*

# Judge Not

When Jesus was asked whether a woman should be condemned for a sin she had committed, he replied, "He that is without sin among you, let him first cast a stone at her." Hearing this, her accusers were forced to examine their own consciences, and one by one they walked away.

No person can know all the underlying, mitigating factors influencing the behavior of others—and therefore cannot judge or condemn them fairly and accurately. In the very act of judging, we close the door to having an open heart and mind—and in ways become like the person we judge.

Similar to the principles Better to Examine the Self and the Golden Rule, this concept is an expression of the underlying truth that we should always be attentive to assisting others on their paths to understanding, rather than acting as impediments.

Philosophers and scholars have analyzed this principle for thousands of years, but for those who are aware of their own shortcomings and are thereby reluctant to judge others, the meaning is simple and clear.

# Judge Not

Judge not, and ye shall not be judged: condemn not, and ye shall not be condemned: forgive, and ye shall be forgiven.

*Christianity*

Judge not thy neighbor till thou art in his place.

*Judaism*

Judge not thy neighbor.

*Buddhism*

Follow that which is revealed to thee, and persevere with patience until God shall judge; for he is the best judge.

*Islam*

All religions teach that we should love one another, that we should seek out our own shortcomings before we presume to condemn the faults of others. . . . Who are we to judge?

*Bahá'í*

# Love Your Enemies

This central principle was commented upon directly by the founder of each religion. Jesus instructed his followers not only to love those who love them but those who do not. Mohammed stated that we should do good not only to those who do good to us but also to those who oppress us. And Vyasa, in the Hindu scripture the Mahabharata, insisted that all people should love both friend and foe alike.

The enlightened teachers of every religion have seen the causes, consequences, and possibilities of human affairs in the broadest possible perspective. They have realized that disagreements and animosities between people are symptoms of deeper, underlying problems. Without awareness of the Oneness of all people, even petty grievances can escalate into confrontations, and the resolution of surface differences is an endless task. One problem leads to another, and all difficulties become so seemingly interwoven that resolution becomes impossible.

Oppression will never be ended by opposing it with oppression. War will never be ended by warring against it. The scriptures of the world's religions are very clear on this point. Only by becoming aware of our common heritages can we evolve beyond the limited vision that results in conflicts. Only by becoming aware of the Divine within us—the Divine that is within every person—can the basis for lasting peace and harmony be established.

# Love Your Enemies

Love your enemies, do good to them which hate you.

Christianity

Do not say that if people do good to us, we will do good to them; and if people oppress us, we will oppress them; but determine that if people do you good, you will do good to them; and if they oppress you, you will not oppress them.

Islam

Confucius was asked, "What do you say of the remark, 'Repay enmity with kindness?' " And he replied, "How then would you repay kindness? Repay kindness with kindness, and enmity with justice."

Confucianism

If thine enemy be hungry, give him bread to eat; and if he be thirsty, give him water to drink.

*Judaism*

Conquer a man who never gives by gifts; subdue untruthful men by truthfulness; vanquish an angry man by gentleness; and overcome the evil man by goodness.

*Hinduism*

Subdue wrath by forgiveness . . . fraud by straightforwardness.

*Jainism*

# Wisdom Is More Precious Than Riches

Wisdom is not a vague quality of mind. It is not a mood of resignation or detachment. Wisdom is a combination of experience and awareness that gives great dynamism to every activity undertaken. It is emotional strength, mental clarity, and intuitive power.

Wisdom allows a person to evaluate experiences of the past in such a clear and decisive manner that upcoming chances for misfortune are minimized—or even avoided altogether. It allows a person to look so deeply into present activities that glimpses of the future can be seen.

In the fullest sense, wisdom is a state of consciousness. Wisdom dawns when a person experiences the connection of his or her individual awareness with the Infinite. Then life is lived in the light of God, and all undertakings are completely successful and fulfilling.

# Wisdom Is More Precious Than Riches

Riches are not from an abundance of worldly goods, but from a contented mind.

*Islam*

Lay not up for yourselves treasures upon earth, where moth and rust doth corrupt, and where thieves break through and steal. But lay up for yourselves treasures in heaven, where neither moth nor rust doth corrupt, and where thieves do not break through and steal: for where your treasure is, there will your heart be also.

*Christianity*

How much better is it to get wisdom than gold! and to get understanding rather than silver!

*Judaism*

# Wisdom Is More Precious
# Than Riches

The real treasure is laid up by a man or woman through charity and piety, temperance and self-control . . . The treasure thus hid is secure, and does not pass away.

*Buddhism*


Knowledge is the best treasure that a man can secretly hoard in life. Learning is the revered of the revered. It is learning alone that enables a man to better the conditions of his friends and relations. Knowledge is the holiest of the holies, the god of gods, and commands respect of crowned heads; shorn of it man is but an animal.

*Hinduism*

# Man Does Not Live
# by Bread Alone

Bread cannot satisfy spiritual hunger. Yet that yearning often goes unrecognized. We seek meaning and fulfillment in worldly activities, neglecting the sustenance of our souls.

The blessings of life are deeper than what can be appreciated by the senses or the mind. Every aspect of life swirls with rhythms of the Divine. All activities, all successes, all well-being and happiness have their basis in an unfathomable Spirit that sustains us even when we are not aware of it. This is the nourishment that we all seek.

The fullest expression of the Divine is found in loving relationships between people. Life is nourished by kindness, by concern for others, by forgiving, by sharing, and by caring for all of God's creatures. We do not live by material bread alone. We live by a deeper power, one that creates and supports all the functions of life.

# Man Does Not Live
# by Bread Alone

Man shall not live by bread alone, but by every word of God.

*Christianity*

Man lives not by material bread alone.

*Hinduism*

Make divine knowledge thy food.

*Sikhism*

Man doth not live by bread only, but by every word that proceedeth out of the mouth of the Lord.

*Judaism*

The superior man deliberates upon how he may walk in truth, not upon what he may eat.

*Confucianism*

# Blessed to Forgive

How often does a mother forgive her child? How often did Jesus forgive wrong? How often did Buddha, Mohammed, Shankara, and other enlightened teachers smile forgivingly at the faults of others?

We all will err at some point as we work through the lessons we must learn. Forgiveness can be an unexpectedly cleansing touch given to another, melting any injury. When individuals cultivate an attitude of forgiveness, they help create a pocket of tranquillity in the world.

An attitude of forgiveness fosters channels of love and understanding in the heart. Years of education involving the study of books, laws, and religious precepts cannot culture the intellect and emotions as much as one moment of forgiveness. Only when we practice forgiving others can life blossom into the fullness we desire.

# Blessed to Forgive

The most beautiful thing a man can do is to forgive wrong.

*Judaism*

Then Peter came up and said to him, "Lord, how often shall my brother sin against me, and I forgive him? As many as seven times?" Jesus said to him, "I do not say to you seven times, but seventy times seven."

*Christianity*

He who forgives and makes peace, shall find his reward for it from God.

*Islam*

Where there is forgiveness there is God himself.

*Sikhism*

Recompense injury with kindness.

*Taoism*

Never is hate diminished by hatred;
It is only diminished by love—
    This is an eternal law.

*Buddhism*

# Speak Truth

When a person is untruthful in one area of life, that influence permeates every other area. Untruthfulness creates habits in our personality that ultimately affect everything that we wish to accomplish. We cannot speak lies while at work and then, later in the day, be entirely truthful with our family. Speaking truthfully enhances love and inner growth. If only for the sake of personal fulfillment, we should cultivate truthfulness in all aspects of our lives.

On another level no less important, untruthfulness indicates an ignorance of the underlying Oneness of all life. People lie only when they think that they are separate from others and can make a significant advancement by impeding the progress of others.

Any advantage gained by untruthfulness is temporary at best, because the most fundamental and important activity in life—the achievement of true and lasting fulfillment—is impeded by deceit.

# Speak Truth

Putting away lying, speak every man truth with his neighbor:
for we are members one of another.

*Christianity*

Speak ye every man truth to his neighbor; execute the
judgement of truth and peace in your gates.

*Judaism*

Him I call indeed a Brahmana who utters true speech,
instructive and free from harshness, so that he offends
no one.

*Buddhism*

# Speak Truth

Do not clothe the truth with falsehood; do not knowingly conceal the truth.

*Islam*

Say what is true! Do thy duty. Do not swerve from the truth.

*Hinduism*

A lie can annihilate a thousand truths.

*Ashanti proverb*
*African wisdom*

Sincerity is the way of heaven, and to think how to be sincere is the way of a man. Never was there one possessed of complete sincerity who did not move others. Never was there one without sincerity who was able to move others.

*Confucianism*

# We Are Known by Our Deeds, Not by Our Religion

Since publication of the first edition of *Oneness*, several people have told me that they read aloud the sayings for this principle at the funeral of a family member. In so doing, they wanted to emphasize the positive aspects of their loved one's life, which was demonstrated by his or her care and respect toward others.

Deeds performed solely for the good of others reveals a person's true inner spirituality, even if that person is not outwardly spiritual or a member of an organized religion.

Inner life is the basis for outer activity. Our actions are the mirror of our true inner selves. We need look no deeper than a person's outer activity to see the degree of inner spiritual achievement.

# We Are Known by Our Deeds, Not by Our Religion

God will not ask a man of what race he is. He will ask what he has done.

*Sikhism*

God will render to every man according to his deeds.

*Christianity*

God does not look at your forms and possessions, but He looks at your hearts and deeds.

*Islam*

One hour of good deeds in this world is better than the
whole of life in the world to come.

*Judaism*


Deeds speak louder than words.

*Assiniboine*
*Native American*


No brahmin is a brahmin by birth.
No outcaste is an outcaste by birth.
An outcaste is an outcaste by his deeds.
A brahmin is a brahmin by his deeds.

*Buddhism*

# Be Slow to Anger

The Chinese language has a word for "crisis" that is made up of two separate written symbols—one for "danger" and one for "opportunity." When we can take a calm, detached look at a critical situation, we have the best chance to solve the problem facing us, thereby turning the danger into opportunity and removing an obstacle on our path to success.

Far too often, we become angry when confronted with something that blocks us from achieving a desire. Anger often flares up during the very moments when clarity and objectivity are needed most. In such instances, anger is the enemy of success—and perhaps even of safety. The more we can stand apart from and overcome sudden anger, the greater our chance for success in any undertaking, and the greater our chance for lasting fulfillment in life.

When Mohammed was asked the single most important quality that a person should have, he replied: "Be not angry." This perhaps was because, in the deepest sense, anger separates one person from another, or one group from another.

This is in direct contrast to the Oneness that all scriptures proclaim to be the true state of humanity.

# Be Slow to Anger

He who is slow to anger has great understanding, but he who has a hasty temper exalts folly.

*Judaism*

He who gives up anger attains to God.

*Hinduism*

Let not the sun go down upon your wrath.

*Christianity*

He is not strong who throws others down; but he is strong who controls his anger.

*Islam*

Let us cease from wrath and refrain from angry gestures.

*Shintoism*

He who holds back rising anger like a rolling chariot, him I call a real driver; others only hold the reins.

*Buddhism*

# Follow the Spirit of the Scriptures, Not the Letter

Individual religions, just as different nations and cultures, have unique characteristics. But these characteristics are only the surface aspects. The fundamental principles at the heart of all religions—as those at the core of all cultures and nations—are universal.

For this reason, the letter of the law, or the surface meanings found in the words of the teachings, are not as integral as the spirit of the law, which is universal and shared by all religions and cultures.

# Follow the Spirit of the Scriptures, Not the Letter

The letter killeth, but the spirit giveth life.

*Christianity*

Rather let a letter be uprooted than the Torah be forgotten.

*Judaism*

The Qur'an was sent down in seven dialects, and in every one of its sentences there is an outer and an inner meaning.

*Islam*

A fully enlightened one doth proclaim the truth, both in its letter and in its spirit.

*Buddhism*

# Follow the Spirit of the Scriptures, Not the Letter

Study the words, no doubt, but look
Behind them to the thought they indicate,
And having found it, throw the words away
As chaff when you have sifted out the grain.

*Hinduism*


Let not scholars scrutinize
The language of the wise too closely;
The seers think more of the thought
Than of the words in which 'tis caught.

*Sufism*

# Start When Young
# to Seek Wisdom

Buddha said that every young person naturally wants to affect the world in a positive way. He went on to say, however, that young people should first concentrate on their own inner development, and then turn their attention to helping others.

No one can change anything in the world for the better without first addressing the issues of personal growth. Until we are strong and knowledgeable, even our best intentions will fall short. When we achieve a command of the full range of our mental, emotional, and spiritual potential, we are better able to accomplish all our goals—material and spiritual.

Education is the key to such accomplishment. Generally, education has focused on knowledge in humanities, sciences, and professional training. For complete development, however, two additional aspects are important: study of the collected wisdom of the world's great religions, and prayer accompanied by deep meditation, such as Transcendental Meditation. The first enables a young person to become aware of the most all-inclusive, fundamental principles of spiritual growth. The second enables direct contact with the fundamental spiritual energies of the universe.

These three aspects of education—when applied from a student's earliest age—assure the greatest chance for success, happiness, and harmony in life.

# Start When Young
# to Seek Wisdom

My son, gather instruction from thy youth up; so shalt thou find wisdom till thine old age.

*Judaism*

Knowledge is riches, what one learns in youth is engraven on stone.

*Hinduism*

Seek ye first the kingdom of God, and His righteousness; and all these things shall be added unto you.

*Christianity*

# Start When Young
# to Seek Wisdom

Seek knowledge from the cradle to the grave.

*Islam*

He who, even as a young student, applies himself to the doctrine of truth, illuminates this world like the moon set free from the clouds.

*Buddhism*

# Honor the Elderly

Our culture today does not, overall, follow this precept. Too often we place youth above age, beauty above wisdom, and passing trends above fundamental truths. We unfortunately see the results all around us.

It is not in nature's plan for the elderly to be overly active in society, but they contribute in very important ways to the achievements of a nation. The gathered knowledge of the elderly in practical matters is immense. No person who has specific goals and ambitions should disregard the advice of these experienced individuals.

The more the aspirations of a society are based on achieving the true nature of lasting happiness—which can be gained only through realizing the inner Oneness of all people—the more a society will honor its aged members. Wisdom fills the elderly like water fills a reservoir. For this wellspring to flow, we must maintain a pipeline of respect.

# Honor the Elderly

He who greets and constantly reveres the aged, four things
will increase to him; life, beauty, happiness, power.

*Buddhism*

With the ancient is wisdom; and in length of days
understanding.

*Judaism*

Treat with reverence due to age the elders in your own
family.

*Confucianism*

Rebuke not an elder, but intreat him as a father.

*Christianity*

When an elder speaks, be silent and listen.

*Mohawk*
*Native American*

To honor an old man is to show respect for God.

*Islam*

A village without elders is like a tree without roots.

*Nilotic proverb*
*African wisdom*

# Keep Company with the Wise

Confucius, certainly among the wisest of men, is reputed to have said, "When I hear about wise and knowing people coming into my area, I make every effort to meet them." Similarly, the scriptures of Judaism say, "If thou seest a man of understanding, get thee unto him, and let thy foot wear the steps of his door."

This is the attitude we all should have. We should never become trapped in the self-contented feeling that we know everything we need to know. This is a state of childishness. We should always seek out and meet with the wise who are imbued with experience, observation, and intelligence.

Individuals may be considered wise when they have the ability to obtain maximum achievement and happiness from all undertakings. Learning from such individuals—and wholeheartedly considering their advice—is necessary for anyone desiring success, ongoing health, and avoidance of pitfalls along life's path.

Who are the "wise" in our day and age? This is a crucial question for young people seeking guidance. The wisest individuals among us are scattered among many professions and callings. They may be teachers, religious leaders, doctors, scientists, writers, or businesspeople. Or they may be our own friends, parents, or family members, whose wisdom in certain matters is hidden by our familiarity with them.

# Keep Company with the Wise

He who walks with wise men shall be wise, but the companion of fools will suffer harm.

*Judaism*

In the company of the wise even fools may attain to wisdom.

*Hinduism*

The company of wise, experienced, virtuous, and loving elders is, indeed, a rampart of protection for the young.

*Sufism*

One should follow the good and the wise, as the moon follows the path of the stars.

*Buddhism*

When you meet with a man of worth, seek to attain his level; when you meet with a man of worthless character, examine your own weak points.

*Confucianism*

No one has found God by walking his own way.

*Sikhism*

# There Are Many Paths to God

Expressions of the Divine manifest in varying ways throughout the world—but as shown in this book, the essential principles for spiritual growth are universal.

Truth does not change. It does not vary from religion to religion. We may think that our religions are different, but when tracing them back to their origins, a common source is found.

The basic teachings of each religion that affect the day-to-day lives of religious followers worldwide are in many ways almost identical. Although from different cultural traditions, individuals who follow the ideals of one religion have ethics and moral values that are very similar to those who follow the ideals of other religions—and they find that their paths ultimately converge with a realization of the same ultimate Truth.

# There Are Many Paths to God

There are as many ways to God as souls; as many as the breaths of Adam's sons.

*Islam*

They who worship other gods with faith,
They adore but Me behind those forms;
Many are the paths of men,
But they all in the end come to Me.

*Hinduism*

For as many as are led by the Spirit of God, they are the sons of God.

*Christianity*

# There Are Many Paths to God

Confucius said: "In the world there are many different roads, but the destination is the same."

*Confucianism*

All religions are but stepping-stones back to God.

*Pawnee*
*Native American*

# Seek and Ye Shall Find

Many people today believe that they personally are unable to achieve spiritual growth. They wish to attain inner peace, but they feel that because of their habits and lifestyles, they will never be able to experience such fulfillment.

The scriptures of all religions, however, clearly state that if we truly wish to begin living the blessings that accompany spirituality, our search will not be in vain.

Spirituality is, in its essence, intimate to us. God is very close and is therefore easily known. Even in the midst of our hectic world, we can find inner peace. The journey begins simply by seeking.

# Seek and Ye Shall Find

Seek, and ye shall find. Knock, and it shall be opened
unto you.

*Christianity*

If from thence thou shalt seek the Lord thy God, thou shalt
find him, if thou seek him with all thy heart and with all
thy soul.

*Judaism*

Even he who merely yearns for Divine peace goes beyond
the knowledge found in books.

*Hinduism*

Many millions search for God, and find him in their hearts.

*Sikhism*

Let no man think lightly of goodness, saying in his heart, it will not come nigh unto me. Even by the falling of water-drops a water-pot is filled; the wise man becomes full of good, even if he gather it little by little.

*Buddhism*

He who approaches near to Me one span, I will approach near to him one cubit, and he who approaches near to Me one cubit, I will approach near to him one fathom; and whoever approaches Me walking, I will come to him running.

*Islam*

# Better to Rule the Spirit

The sayings on the following pages emphasize the importance of not degrading one's self for profit or material advancement. There are many opportunities to do so today, just as there have been since the days each of the world's scriptures were written.

Many people may seem to advance toward success by promoting projects that harm others, by turning a blind eye to injustice, by theft or dishonesty, or by distorting legal and political systems. But such success is outward and often only temporary. It comes at the cost of inner calmness and joy. Ultimately, it is in itself an impediment to fulfillment. This truth is expressed in the Hitopadesa of Hinduism: "How can true happiness proceed from wealth improperly gained? In its acquisition, it causes pain. In its loss, misery. In its abundance, folly." The Hadith of Islam states, "If anyone buys a robe for ten coins, even one of which is gained illegally, Allah will not accept prayer from him as long as he wears it." And from the Analects of Confucius: "Wealth and honors that one acquires from injustice are as impermanent as floating clouds."

For the person who wants to experience love, lasting success, and spiritual advancement, this principle has great importance. The world is full of lures, many of which sparkle enticingly while leading us to temporary gains. It is important to avoid even the first steps toward questionable activities, thinking, Just one time won't hurt. It is far too easy to begin feeling that such actions are justified, and that the spiritual path is not worth seeking.

# Better to Rule the Spirit

For what is a man profited, if he shall gain the whole world, and lose his own soul?

*Christianity*

He who is slow to anger is better than the mighty, and he who rules his spirit than he who takes a city.

*Judaism*

If one were to conquer in battle a thousand times a thousand men, he who conquers himself is the greatest warrior.

*Buddhism*

The most excellent jihad is that for the conquest of self.

*Islam*

He who overcomes others is strong; he who overcomes himself is mighty.

*Taoism*

Difficult to conquer is one's self. But when that is conquered, everything is conquered.

*Jainism*

# God Is Forgiving

Without exception, the great teachers of every religion have shown forgiveness to others and have encouraged their followers to maintain a forgiving attitude. Their lives have exemplified the divine quality of forgiveness. Each declared that God, the source of wisdom and virtue, is absolutely forgiving.

This principle is comforting to those suffering as a result of their own activities. The world's scriptures state that we are accountable for our actions and will inevitably suffer when we do wrong to others. But the scriptures say also that God forgives us without reservation when we acknowledge our misdeeds and again set ourselves on the path toward spiritual awareness.

# God Is Forgiving

The Lord your God is gracious and merciful, and will not turn away his face from you, if ye return unto Him.

*Judaism*

He who meets me with sins equivalent to the whole world, I will greet him with forgiveness equal to it.

*Islam*

If we confess our sins, he is faithful and just to forgive us our sins, and to cleanse us from all unrighteousness.

*Christianity*

# God Is Forgiving

However gross his sins, if he will turn
To Me and love Me with unswerving heart,
He is a saint, he has resolved aright
And shall gain everlasting peace.
This I promise, he who loves me shall never perish.

*Hinduism*


If one has done bad deeds of wickedness,
But afterwards repents and mends his way . . .
He, in the long run, will be sure to gain
Good fortune, and will change calamity
Into sweet blessing through the lessons learnt.

*Taoism*


Where there is forgiveness, there is God himself.

*Sikhism*

# Be Loving, as God Is Loving to All

Who knows God's plans for the world? How can we, from our limited vantage point, judge another person's activities?

God showers love and forgiveness on every person day and night, even those branded as criminals by individuals or society. God loves all people, and every scripture says that God most cherishes those who do likewise.

Even when in the course of practical life it becomes necessary for society to correct or punish others, these actions should be founded on the understanding that love and forgiveness are the highest ideals of human relationships.

# Be Loving, as God
# Is Loving to All

As water quenches the thirst of the good and the bad alike, and cleanses them of dust and impurity, so also shall you treat your friend and your foe alike with loving kindness.

*Buddhism*

He maketh His sun to rise on the evil and on the good, and sendeth rain on the just and on the unjust.

*Christianity*

More important is a day of rain than the Resurrection of the Dead, since the Resurrection is for the righteous and not the wicked, whereas rain is for both the righteous and the wicked.

*Judaism*

The earth holds the honest and the wicked. The sun warms the honest and the wicked. The wind blows equally for them. Water cleanses them equally.

*Hinduism*

The highest goodness is like water. Water is beneficent to all things.

*Taoism*

The rain falls on the just and the unjust.

*Hopi
Native American*

My religion is like clouds dropping much rain . . . some falls in the hollows from which mankind are benefited, some falls on high lands from which benefit is not derived.

*Islam*

# Moderation in All Things

Excessive mental or physical activity leads to fatigue. A person's mind and body may be strong and resilient, but regular periods of rest are needed to relieve accumulated fatigue and stress. Mature individuals, who have experienced the results of excessive fatigue in themselves and in others, naturally tend to moderation in their habits. But the young, who feel supplied with unending energy, tend to excess in many ways.

In today's frenetic world, success is equated with long hours of hard work, and stress is accepted as an inevitable side effect. But wear and tear on the body eventually takes its toll. Even the most successful individuals usually advise younger people to take things easier, to keep their bodies healthy, and to enjoy life as they live it.

# Moderation in All Things

He who possesses moderation is lasting and enduring.

*Taoism*

Commit no excess; do nothing injurious . . . pleasures should not be carried to excess.

*Confucianism*

He who avoids extremes in eating and fasting,
In sleep and waking, and in work and play,
He wins balance, peace, and joy.

*Hinduism*

Let your moderation be known unto all men.

*Christianity*

# Moderation in All Things

If a man oversteps the limits of moderation, he pollutes his body and mind.

*Shintoism*

Observe moderation in all you do, and if that is not possible, try to be near moderation.

*Islam*

# Pride Goes Before a Fall

Excessive pride hinders advancement and contentment. It blinds us to the necessity of careful consideration and consultation before any undertaking, and it severs our inner awareness from the ongoing connection with the Divine, which is the source of all intelligence, organization, and fulfillment.

Pride is a part of life; it is natural to feel good about achievements. But excessive pride detaches a person from the very source of success. A person may feel, I alone am responsible for this. But every undertaking has innumerable critical aspects that are beyond the control of individuals. To take advantage of these, we should continually remain thankful that God created the conditions for success. We should always maintain a feeling of goodwill toward others, respect for national laws, and gratitude to God for favors received.

# Pride Goes Before a Fall

Pride goes before destruction, and a haughty spirit before a fall.

*Judaism*

Pride bringeth loss; humility, increase; this is the way of Heaven. He comes to ruin who says that others do not equal him.

*Confucianism*

Pride is the very gateway to defeat.

*Hinduism*

Be clothed with humility, for God resisteth the proud, and giveth grace to the humble.

*Christianity*

Surely God loveth not the proud and boastful.

*Islam*

Humility is the root of honor.

*Taoism*

# The Soul Is Eternal

Several years ago, a close friend visited my wife and me. Every morning, he woke early and walked on the beach. Usually he was quite talkative when he returned, but one morning he was silent and slightly withdrawn. Later, I spoke with him about it.

"I was walking along the shore," he said, "enjoying the waves as they lapped up. One a little larger, the next a little smaller.

"Then I had the thought that the waves never stop. I realized that they've crashed on the beach like that for millions, even billions of years—and that they'll continue for billions after I'm gone. I've known that before, of course, but it suddenly seemed so clear. The thought comforted me, because I felt that I would always be a part of it, in some way . . ."

His voice trailed off. Our conversation drifted on to other subjects, but I knew what had happened. We were quiet then—listening to the wind pick up, blowing in from the water. Even though we all went to bed late that night, my wife

The soul, after its separation from the body, will continue to progress until it attaineth the presence of God.

*Bahá'í*

Birthless and deathless and changeless remains the soul, dead though the house of it seems.

*Hinduism*

The grave is the first station in the journey to eternity.

*Islam*

# In the Beginning

Every religion describes the source of the universe as a vast and powerful force that is infinitely creative and dynamic, yet filled with inexhaustible peace and silence. The beginning of the universe is described almost as a meditation, as consciousness moving and forming material creation from its own transcendent nature.

These expressions of the source of the universe are descriptions of the qualities of God. Can we truly imagine this vastness? Each religion has made an attempt to describe this unimaginable power and intelligence. As stated in the Sikh religion: "In describing him there would never be an end. Millions of men give millions upon millions of descriptions of Him, but they fail to describe Him."

# In the Beginning

In the beginning there was indescribable darkness;
Then was not earth or heaven, naught but God's unequaled
  Order.
Then was not day, or night, or moon, or sun; God was
  meditating on the void.

*Sikhism*


In the beginning there was neither existence nor
  nonexistence;
Then there was neither sky nor atmosphere above . . .
Then was there neither death nor immortality,
Then was there neither day, nor night, nor light, nor
  darkness,
Only the existent One breathed calmly, self-contained.

*Hinduism*

# In the Beginning

In the beginning God created the heaven and the earth.
And the earth was without form, and void; and the darkness
was upon the face of the deep. And the Spirit of God moved
upon the face of the waters. And God said, Let there be
light: and there was light.

*Judaism*

In the beginning was the Word, and the Word was with
God, and the Word was God. The same was in the
beginning with God. All things were made by him; and
without him was not any thing made that was made.

*Christianity*

There was something undefined and complete, coming into existence before Heaven and Earth. How still it was and formless, standing alone, and undergoing no change, reaching everywhere and in no danger of being exhausted. It may be regarded as the Mother of all things.

*Taoism*

He is the first and the last; the Seen and the Hidden; and He knoweth all things! It is He who in six days created the Heavens and the Earth, then ascended His throne.

*Islam*

# God Created All Things

The incomprehensible power that created the billions of galaxies scattered across the universe—each with billions upon billions of stars—also created the infinitely subtle existence of subatomic particles, many of which cannot be seen even with the most powerful microscopes.

The vast intelligence that established and guides the movement of the cosmos also supports the flowing of our own delicate emotions, such as love, devotion, faith, and joy.

Where in the physical universe does the emotion of love exist? Where is a memory? Where are the sensations of joy, of sadness, of longing? They exist in a dimension or space that we certainly did not create. God has made these, just as he has made us.

We, in our desire to control and create, attempt to emulate God's work. But we forever fall short. As stated in the Hadith sayings of the Islamic scriptures, "Let man try to create an atom! Let him try to create a grain of barley!"

# God Created All Things

Every house is built by some one, but the builder of all things is God.

*Christianity*

This universe hath sprung from the Lord. In him it is established. He is the Cause of Creation.

*Hinduism*

All things originate from heaven.

*Confucianism*

It is he who made the earth by his power, who established the world by his wisdom, and by his understanding stretched out the heavens.

*Judaism*

# God Created All Things

Praise be to God, who created the heavens and the earth, and ordained the darkness and the light! He it is who created you.

*Islam*

God is ever true. He is the true Lord. He who made this world is and always shall be. Behold! His handiwork attests his greatness.

*Sikhism*

We do not see God, but all we see are His works.

*Ethiopia*
*African wisdom*

# God Is Beyond Comprehension

However deeply we examine any aspect of nature, we find an infinitely complex pattern of intelligence and orderliness. In our small way we seek understanding of the vastness, but the wider our range of knowledge becomes, the more the unknown expands before us. Our intellect and senses cannot pierce to the depth or expanse of the universe.

A story from the Upanishads, a scripture of ancient India, comes to mind when considering the mysteries of the universe. To instill within a pupil a sense of God's incomprehensibility, an enlightened teacher instructed the young man to break open a banyan seed, which when full grown is an enormous, sprawling, majestic tree. The pupil did as instructed, and when the seed was opened, the teacher asked, "What do you find?"

"Nothing," the student answered, "the seed is hollow inside."

"Now you have begun to explore the great mystery of God. From the nothingness inside this tiny seed the mighty banyan tree springs. Just so, from the silent transcendence of God springs the entire universe. How this happens, we can never understand. We can only appreciate it, and wonder."

# God Is Beyond Comprehension

God does great things which we cannot comprehend.

Judaism

O the depth of the riches both of the wisdom and knowledge of God! how unsearchable are his judgments, and his ways past finding out!

Christianity

Thou, God, art beyond all thought, conception, guess, imagination, yea, and far beyond all we have spoken, heard, or read in books.

Sufism

How pure and still is the Supreme Being!
How deep and unfathomable!

*Taoism*

If all the trees that are upon the earth were to become pens,
and if God should after that swell the sea into seven seas of
ink, His words would not be exhausted: of a truth God is
Mighty, Wise.

*Islam*

Were the earth to become paper, the forests pens, and the
wind a writer, the end of the endless one could not be
described.

*Sikhism*

# Be Content

Expressing the sentiments of all religions, the Hadith sayings of Islam state, "True wealth is not in vast riches, but in self-contentment."

It is easy to lose appreciation for the simplicity of life. We tend to think that we want and need certain things, and that we have to work extremely hard to get them. But throughout history it has been proven that wealth—and the trappings that surround it—do not necessarily lead to contentment.

Being content with one's life does not mean becoming inactive or uninterested in the world. Contentment, in its fullest sense, is a state of inner awareness that enables a person to maintain inner calmness even in the midst of success and failure.

# Be Content

Do not be anxious about your life, what you shall eat or what you shall drink; nor about your body, what you shall put on. Is not life more than food, and the body more than clothing? Look at the birds of the air: they neither sow nor reap nor gather into barns, and yet your heavenly Father feeds them.

*Christianity*

God provideth everyone with his daily food; why, O man, art thou afraid?

*Sikhism*

Contentment is the greatest wealth.

*Buddhism*

# Be Content

A tranquil mind gives life.

*Judaism*

Contentment is the root of happiness, and discontent the root of misery.

*Hinduism*

Every little yielding to anxiety is a step away from the natural heart of man.

*Shintoism*

# Seek the Good of the World

When we admire a rose, our attention is drawn to the beauty and softness of the petals, not to the sharpness of the thorns. When we eat an orange, we discard the bitter outer skin in favor of the sweet inner juice. It is such with many things in life; the better part of wisdom is the ability to see the good of the world in the midst of the bad.

Cultivating the habit of appreciating goodness allows us to grow in inner peace and happiness. The world is very dark for those who see the bad and miss the good, because the good is a more complete expression of the Divine. Also, appreciating the good encourages goodness to grow, both in ourselves and in others. By encouraging the good in a person, in a nation, or in a religion, we nourish their finest aspects and give them the best chance to blossom into fullness.

# Seek the Good of the World

As the ant collects grains of sugar from among grains of salt, so should you seek the good in the world from among the bad.

*Hinduism*

Sift out the good from the many things you hear, and follow them; sift out the good from the many things you see and remember them.

*Confucianism*

Observe all the white around you, but remember all the black that is there.

*Taoism*

Our eyes may see some uncleanliness, but let not our minds see things that are not clean. Our ears may hear some uncleanliness, but let not our minds hear things that are not clean.

*Shintoism*

Whatsoever things are true, whatsoever things are honest, whatsoever things are just, whatsoever things are pure, whatsoever things are lovely, whatsoever things are of good report; if there be any virtue, and if there be any praise, think on these things.

*Christianity*

# Speak Gently

A word fitly spoken can uplift the soul. Similarly, a word thoughtlessly spoken can scar a person for life. In many ways, speech is a gross and superficial means of communication, because it is not possible at any given moment to be fully aware of another person's inner thoughts and needs. For this reason it is always best to speak gently and with consideration. Even truth should be tempered with sweetness so no injury is done to the delicate feelings of others.

Graciousness to others and care for their well-being are the marks of a spiritually developed person. As we would have people speak gently and with understanding to us in our times of need, so we should do to them.

# Speak Gently

Don't speak harshly to anyone, lest others will speak to you
in the same way.

*Buddhism*

Let your speech always be gracious, seasoned with salt,
so that you may know how you ought to answer every one.

*Christianity*

Utter not one disagreeable word, since the true Lord is in all
men. Distress no one's heart; every heart is a priceless jewel.

*Sikhism*

Harsh words hurt more than a poisonous arrow.

*Nilotic proverb*
*African wisdom*

# Speak Gently

Words that cause no woe, words always true, gentle and pleasing words—these mark the true religious speech.

*Hinduism*

Be modest in thy bearing, and speak with words of gentleness.

*Islam*

An angry word is like striking with a knife.

*Hopi*
*Native American*

A word fitly spoken is like apples of gold in a setting of silver.

*Judaism*

# Do Not Look
# for Faults in Others

When a person becomes overly irritated with shortcomings in others, it indicates that superficial aspects of life are being focused on, and that deeper, more meaningful aspects are being missed. Life progresses toward truth and rightness, but individuals have shortcomings and make mistakes on the path.

When we become annoyed with others and tend to find fault, we should question what it is, within us, that causes such irritation. Differences of personality always exist, but when the underlying Oneness of all people is appreciated, the inherent, often hidden beauty within each person is revealed.

This sentiment is beautifully expressed by a saying of Confucius: "To be in one's inmost heart in kindly sympathy with all things; to love all men; to allow no selfish thoughts—this is the nature of benevolence and righteousness."

# Do Not Look for
# Faults in Others

The disease of men is that they neglect their own field, and go to weed the fields of others, and that what they require of others is great, while what they lay upon themselves is light.

*Confucianism*

He who sees his own faults has no time to see the faults of others.

*Islam*

Find fault with thyself rather than with others.

*Shintoism*

Wherein thou judgest another, thou condemnest thyself; for thou that judgest doest the same things.

*Christianity*

How couldst thou forget thine own faults and busy thyself with the faults of others?

*Bahá'í*

To attempt to correct another person's virtue while one's own virtue is clouded, is to set one's own virtue a task for which it is inadequate.

*Taoism*

# The Blessing of Charity

Every mature, responsible person feels an inner lack when hearing of the suffering of others. Television, radio, and newspapers keep us in constant contact with events worldwide, continually reminding us of the material disparity between nations and people.

"Above all things have fervent charity among yourselves: for charity shall cover the multitude of sins," says Christianity in the Holy Bible. This is perhaps more urgent today than ever, as inequalities increase.

Many poorer regions of the world today feel strongly that the more advanced nations do not adequately share their technology, agricultural systems, and medical resources. Charity in this light involves more than the mere offering of money.

Without such assistance, inequalities may grow to such dimensions that civilization will be threatened. It is vital to maintain the blessing of charity—even when it seems a hardship. Without the practice of charity, an individual's life grows stale and unfeeling, and a nation's existence becomes self-centered and insecure.

# The Blessing of Charity

Give to him that asketh thee, and from him that would borrow of thee turn not thou away.

*Christianity*

The Prophet said: "Give in charity and do not withold it, otherwise Allah will withhold it back from you."

*Islam*

He that hath pity upon the poor lendeth unto the Lord; and that which he hath given will He pay him again.

*Judaism*

# The Blessing of Charity

As a full jar overflowing pours out the liquid and keeps back nothing, even so shall your charity be without reserve—as a jar overturned.

*Buddhism*

Bounteous is he who gives to the beggar who comes to him in want of food and feeble.

*Hinduism*

Charity belongs to the most honorable nobility of Heaven, and is the quiet home where man should dwell.

*Confucianism*

# The Blessing of Hospitality

"Use hospitality one to another without grudging," says the New Testament of the Holy Bible. "Let a man honor his guest," says the Hadith traditions of Islam. And "The guest is God," says the Vedic tradition of Hinduism.

How many times has each of us longed for hospitality or needed assistance while traveling far from home? How often would a simple offering of help have eased our burden? The kind and thoughtful person watches for opportunities to help others. Many people do not ask for assistance, but their need may be very great.

Practiced in many traditions as a way to increase spiritual progress, hospitality is a principle central to all religions. We are all travelers in this world. The more we can lighten the load for others, the easier our own path becomes.

# The Blessing of Hospitality

Neither vex a stranger, nor oppress him: for ye were strangers.

Judaism

Hospitality should be shown to even one's foe when he comes to one's house.

Hinduism

Then consider that visiting friends are a necessary custom, whatever they be, on foot, or mounted. And if it be an enemy, this act of kindness is still good, for many an enemy by kindness becomes a friend.

Islam

Let brotherly love continue. Be not forgetful to entertain strangers: for thereby some have entertained angels unawares.

*Christianity*

In all the world there is no such thing as a stranger.

*Shintoism*

# Give Without Thought
# of Reward

When a mother gives to her child, no conditions accompany the giving. Love spontaneously flows, and this nurturing is the source of all growth and strength. Similarly, the enlightened founders of every religion gave endlessly of themselves, asking nothing in return. Without exception, their lives were models of giving and are standards of inspiration for us all.

When we give to others in a pure, innocent spirit, our hearts become cultured in a profound way. Those who give in such a spontaneous manner experience great meaning in life. They realize the preciousness of every moment. They transcend the petty squabbles of the world and achieve a higher vision, realizing that every person is a spark of the Divine.

# Give Without Thought
# of Reward

A gift is pure when it is given from the heart . . . and when
nothing is expected in return.

*Hinduism*

If you give alms publicly, it is well; but it is better to give
them secretly. God knows what you do.

*Islam*

Do not your alms before men, to be seen of them: otherwise
ye have no reward of your Father which is in heaven.

*Christianity*

# Give Without Thought
## of Reward

True charity is practiced in secret. The best type of charity is where the person who gives does not know who receives it; and the person who receives does not know who gave it.

Judaism

Extend your help without seeking reward. Give to others and do not regret or begrudge your liberality. Those who are thus are good.

Taoism

# Give and You Shall Receive Again

This precept may seem in direct contrast to Give Without Thought of Reward. The world's scriptures, however, often give what may seem to be conflicting advice. This is because no single instruction can apply to all people in all circumstances. Just as no single food is completely beneficial to every person, so no counsel is universally applicable.

When encountering seemingly conflicting advice within a scripture, take to heart what you feel most directly applies to you at the time. Heed the words that strike your heart; disregard those that seem out of place or untimely.

This particular saying could be beneficial to a person who needs to understand that charity brings tangible rewards in the future. This reward could be in forms other than money: happiness, unexpected encouragement, love, or health.

# Give and You Shall
# Receive Again

Give, and it shall be given unto you . . . For with the same
measure that ye mete withal it shall be measured to you
again.

*Christianity*


Cast your bread upon the waters: for you will find it after
many days.

*Judaism*


Those who give in charity have lent to Allah a goodly loan.

*Islam*

If you would take, you must first give; this is the beginning of intelligence.

*Taoism*

Give, and your wealth shall grow; give, and you shall more safely keep the wealth you have.

*Hinduism*

What goes out from thee comes back to thee again.

*Confucianism*

# The Goodness of Wealth

There is no limit to the supply of good things given to us by God. When a person feels that there is such a limit, all work becomes a competition to divide up the existing supply of wealth and goods. In that moment, a person begins to breed struggle and discomfort throughout society. Success secured in a sense of competition with others is never satisfying. It does not bring inner fulfillment. When success is seized at what is considered the expense of others, there is always the sense that it can be lost or stolen.

The spiritually aware person acts in accordance with the laws of society and with the deeper, fundamental laws common to all religious teachings. Such action brings the Divine—which exists in great fullness within each person—out into the world. This allows individuals to raise themselves above the competitive plane and to work and live on the creative plane, where there is never a lack, where each individual is a creator of new wealth, not a taker or divider of existing wealth.

For a person who has gained wealth in this way, it is natural to support humanitarian causes. With the awareness that there is no lack in the world, the fear of loss has no chance to gain a foothold.

# The Goodness of Wealth

In the house of the righteous is much treasure: but in the revenues of the wicked is trouble.

*Judaism*

Wealth, properly employed, is a blessing; and one may lawfully endeavor to increase it by honest means.

*Islam*

Every good deed will bear its fruit to men; there is no escape from the effects of one's actions. Through riches and the highest pleasures the soul has the reward for its virtues.

*Jainism*

He who does what is proper, who takes the yoke upon him and exerts himself, will acquire wealth.

*Buddhism*

Riches and honors acquired by unrighteousness are to me as a floating cloud.

*Confucianism*

Honor is at the very root of wealth.

*Hinduism*

# Knowledge Is
# the Basis for Success

Speaking in broad terms, there are two levels of knowledge: outer knowledge, involving technical understanding of objects or events in the relative world, and inner knowledge, involving moral and spiritual growth. Both are necessary for progress. The lack of either impedes the development of life both for individuals and society as a whole.

Every great achievement—every invention; every business success; and every piece of art, literature, or music—begins as a quiet thought in an individual's mind. To express such ideas and bring them forth into solid reality, technical knowledge is required. One of a generation's greatest gifts to the following generation is the accumulation and refinement of technical knowledge.

Underlying all advancement is the collective wisdom of the world's great religions. Not in an abstract sense, but in a very practical way, the understanding of the values of love, peace, harmony, and spiritual unity establish meaning for life.

These values form the framework upon which achievements based on technical knowledge can blossom. Even the greatest outward success would mean little in a world empty of spiritual values. Spiritual growth takes place within each individual—very privately and quietly—but the collective result is the advancement of the world's wholeness.

# Knowledge Is
# the Basis for Success

Let all things be done decently and in order.

*Christianity*

Knowledge crowns endeavor with success.

*Buddhism*

By wisdom a house is built, and by understanding it is established; by knowledge the rooms are filled with all precious and pleasant riches.

*Judaism*

Men of superior mind busy themselves first getting at the root of things; when they succeed, the right course is open to them.

*Confucianism*

With knowledge man rises to the heights of goodness and a noble position, associates with the sovereigns of this world, and attains the perfection of happiness in the next world.

*Islam*

# Perseverance Is
# the Key to Success

Few personal qualities are more important for success than perseverance. This is true both in the pursuit of worldly success and in the development of inner spirituality. Many undertakings that seem simple and straightforward at their beginning become complex and difficult at various stages of development. This is true of artistic pursuits, scientific study and research, business ventures, personal relationships, and even spiritual activities. From earliest childhood, a person should be encouraged to stay with something to the end, no matter how difficult or complex it becomes. In this way, the full potential of every activity can be realized.

This principle illustrates the practical value of studying the world's religious scriptures. People of all races and cultures have turned to these great texts not only for inspiration and spiritual guidance, but also for practical suggestions about specific situations encountered in day-to-day life. The world may seem more complicated today than it was in the times of the great spiritual teachers, but their words address situations relevant to us all.

# Perseverance Is
# the Key to Success

As the stone mountain, firmly based, quails not before the tempest, but abides in its place, so also shall you abide in your resolution once resolved.

*Buddhism*

The plans of the diligent lead surely to abundance, but every one who is hasty comes only to want.

*Judaism*

Confucius said: "Do not be impatient, and do not look for small advantages. If you are impatient, you will not be thorough. If you look to small advantages, you will never accomplish great things."

*Confucianism*

Let your footsteps be slow and steady that you stumble not.

*Shintoism*

Do not desist from work: that treasure indeed will follow upon it. Beware lest you become a slave to "If," saying to yourself, "If I had only done this or the other."

*Islam*

People are constantly spoiling projects that are only one step from completion.

*Taoism*

# We Create Our Own Destiny

We are created by God, a force that transcends understanding, and many unseen factors help determine our successes and failures. Yet we have free will, and our own choices at every step make us ultimately responsible for whatever befalls us.

At moments of choice, we need to favor wise counsel above hasty decisions. Something may seem to glitter with charm, yet upon deeper consideration will be understood as harmful or even destructive to our destiny.

To achieve what we desire in life, it is helpful to study and understand the teachings of the great religions. These unfailing guides offer proven, well-thought-out counsel. When reaching a crucial turning point in our lives, what would we not give to have Jesus, Buddha, Confucius, or Moses to speak with and ask questions of? Yet they are with us now—or at least their essential wisdom is—in the scriptures of the great religions.

# We Create Our Own Destiny

He shall reward every man according to his work.

*Christianity*

The pure and impure stand and fall by their own deeds.

*Buddhism*

Unto thee, O Lord!, belongeth mercy: for thou renderest to every man according to his work.

*Judaism*

Calamity and happiness are in all cases men's own making.

*Confucianism*

# We Create Our Own Destiny

Whatever of misfortune falls on one,
Of one's own doings it is the result.
The atom's weight of good that you have done,
That you shall see come back to you again.

*Islam*

Everyone reaps the fruit of their own deeds.

*Hinduism*

# The Love of Good Works

The more spiritually aware people become, the more clearly they understand that inner contentment depends on performing good works for others. The simplicity and straightforwardness of a person who seeks good for others has a profound effect on every level of existence—externally for others, and internally for the person producing good.

A person who desires to enjoy the inner fruits of good works has risen to a high level of understanding, not only of his or her own religion but of the most universal spiritual laws, which are shared by all religions. The scriptures of every religion are overflowing with wisdom that enables individuals to grow to this advanced state of life, which is filled with great satisfaction and contentment. It does not matter which religion a person follows. All who seek the highest good for others find the most complete contentment within themselves.

# The Love of Good Works

The virtuous man delights and rejoices when he sees the good results of his own work.

*Buddhism*

Let a person continually take pleasure in truth, in justice, in laudable practices and in purity.

*Hinduism*

Blessed are they which do hunger and thirst after righteousness, for they shall be filled.

*Christianity*

Better than the one who knows what is right is he who loves what is right.

*Confucianism*

A man asked the Prophet what was the mark whereby a man might know the reality of his faith. He said, "If thou derive pleasure from the good which thou hast done, and be grieved for the evil which thou hast committed, thou art a true believer."

*Islam*

His delight is in the law of the Lord; and in his law doth he meditate day and night.

*Judaism*

# God Is Found in the Heart

The immortal abides within the heart of each person. This quiet presence is always within us. It is the still voice at the center of our souls. It is the innermost awareness that guides and supports us during our most trying moments.

In today's world, many of us have lost contact with this inner silence. In every direction we turn, silence has been lost. Television and radio announcers seem to abhor silence. They fill every second with noise and endless talk, not listening to answers after they ask questions, not allowing their audience a moment to reflect.

In such incessant frenzy, the loud and rude drown out the silent and thoughtful. The brash elbow out the considerate. Ultimately, this makes life more jarring and abrasive, and the simple silence that is the basis for contentment seems remote and even meaningless.

To overcome this, find a silent spot and sit quietly, absorbing yourself in prayer or deep meditation. In doing so, you'll inevitably find that your desires are quite simple and basic.

The world's tangled problems often make it seem that attaining personal fulfillment is complex and difficult. But it is a simple and natural thing, because nothing is more intimate to us than God.

# God Is Found in the Heart

If we keep unperverted the human heart—which is like unto heaven and received from earth—that is God.

*Shintoism*

God is concealed in every heart, his light is in every heart.

*Sikhism*

Know ye not that ye are the temple of God, and that the Spirit of God dwelleth in you?

*Christianity*

God is the light of all lights and luminous beyond all darkness of our ignorance. He is the knowledge and the object of knowledge. He is seated in the hearts of all.

*Hinduism*

The heart of him who knows, and so believes with full assurance, is the throne of God.

*Islam*

May He abide always within my heart,
The Supreme Self, the One God of all gods.

*Jainism*

# Man Proposes, God Disposes

During a private conversation between us, Mother Teresa told me that she greatly appreciated the comparisons between religions in *Oneness*. They were valuable and important, she said, because they could foster understanding and harmony between people. Near the end of the conversation she told me, "I pray that this book accomplishes what God wants it to."

What she meant by this, she explained, is that God has a special purpose for every action. People's individual desires and egos, however, often distort this. Her prayer meant that she hoped people would not thwart or alter God's intention for the message of *Oneness*.

Her words also indicate that by allowing God to determine the course of events in any worthwhile undertaking, the greatest chance for success is assured. Although our personal thoughts, plans, and activities play an integral role in God's working for the success of projects, it is necessary to "let go" even while remaining attuned with God. In this way, our desires can be supported most fully and efficiently by the Almighty's universal awareness, which extends beyond our own limited comprehension.

# Man Proposes, God Disposes

Effort is mine, to grant success is God's. Man should propose, only God can dispose.

*Islam*

Know that all reliance on man is vain;
It is God alone who bestoweth.

*Sikhism*

I have planted . . . but God gave the increase.

*Christianity*

Though men may spin their cunning schemes—God knows who shall lose or win.

*Hinduism*

God knows the things of tomorrow.

*Burundi*
*African wisdom*

A man's heart deviseth his way: but the Lord directeth his steps.

*Judaism*

# He Who Slays Anyone

The basis of all religious thought finds summation in a saying from the Bhagavad Gita, one of the central Hindu scriptures. "When a man sees that the Divine in himself is the same Divine in everyone, he hurts not himself by hurting others." When this profound truth of human existence is understood, and when it becomes the basis for all action by all people, the world will enter an age of heaven on earth.

Anyone who hurts or kills another person does not have this awareness, and no amount of rehabilitation or punishment can reestablish correct behavior—unless accompanied by the growth of inner understanding.

# He Who Slays Anyone

Whoever destroys one life, Scripture ascribes it to him as though he had destroyed the whole world: and whoever saves one life, Scripture ascribes it to him as though he had saved the whole world.

*Judaism*

He who slayeth anyone . . . shall be as though he had slain all mankind; but he who saveth a life shall be as though he had saved all mankind alive.

*Islam*

All they that take the sword shall perish with the sword.

*Christianity*

# He Who Slays Anyone

All men tremble at punishment and all men fear death, for
all life is dear; remember that you are like them and do not
kill nor cause slaughter.

*Buddhism*

All living beings hate pain; therefore do not injure them or
kill them. This is the essence of wisdom: not to kill
anything.

*Jainism*

# Avoid Doing What
# You Know to Be Wrong

Parents continually protect their young children from harming themselves or others. Gradually, each person grows in the awareness of right and wrong and becomes able to make mature decisions. Until that time, a person needs to be guided by a wiser and more experienced teacher.

When individuals begin to take responsibility for themselves, the most all-inclusive rule of behavior is to avoid doing what is known to be wrong. This principle works in all situations and at all times. When cultivated, it becomes a habit that allows us to avoid injuring ourselves and others and helps us to avoid suffering. By listening to our own inner knowledge of right and wrong, and by acting upon what we know to be right, obstacles are removed from our path.

# Avoid Doing What
# You Know to Be Wrong

Do nothing which appears wicked in your own eyes.

*Judaism*

When anything pricketh your conscience, forsake it.

*Islam*

Knowing the truth, one should live up to it.

*Jainism*

Whoever knows what is right to do and fails to do it, for him
it is sin.

*Christianity*

If knowing your duty and task, you bid duty and task go by—
that is sin.

*Hinduism*

Let a man avoid doing what his sense of righteousness tells
him to avoid. This is the most direct and simplest way to act
correctly in all circumstances.

*Confucianism*

# Definitions of Religion

Within the scripture of each religion is the definition of religion itself. These essences, or self-referral descriptions, clearly express the practices, beliefs, and understanding that enable a person to build a firm and positive structure in life.

The world's religious scriptures are wonderful guides, offering us the chance to "keep company with the wise," as though the great spiritual teachers were still living among us and sharing their good counsel.

Religion in this sense is very practical. It is not limiting to our satisfaction and fulfillment. Rather, it enables us to evolve to the highest point of human consciousness, wherein Oneness is achieved with all the laws of nature. It allows us to avoid mistakes, to take the path of growth and achievement, and to answer the urgent and vital questions that ultimately arise.

# Definitions of Religion

Wherein does religion consist? It consists in doing as little harm as possible, in doing good in abundance, in the practice of love, of compassion, of truthfulness and purity, in all the walks of life.

*Buddhism*

All the law is fulfilled in one word, even in this; Thou shalt love they neighbour as thyself.

*Christianity*

True religion is to love, as God loves them, all things, whether great or small.

*Hinduism*

# Definitions of Religion

To be a cause of healing to every sick one; a comforter for
every sorrowful one; a pleasant water for every thirsty one;
a heavenly table for every hungry one; a guide for every
seeker . . . a light for every lamp; a herald to every
yearning one for the kingdom of God.

*Bahá'í*

Pity the misfortunes of others; rejoice in the well-being of
others; help those who are in want; save those in danger;
rejoice at the success of others; and sympathize with their
reverses, even as though you were in their place.

*Taoism*

What actions are most excellent? To gladden the heart of a
human being, to feed the hungry, to help the afflicted, to
lighten the sorrow of the sorrowful, and to remove the
wrongs of the injured.

*Islam*

# All Religions Inspired by God

The scriptures of nearly every religion proclaim that the religion's founder was inspired directly by God. The ancient Vedic sages—Manu, Vyasa, and Shankara, among others—have been revered by millions of Hindus as direct channels of God to mankind.

The Buddhist scriptures proclaim Buddha as the enlightened knower of the ultimate reality. Abraham, Moses, and other founders of Judaism are described in the Old Testament of the Holy Bible as speaking directly with God. The New Testament declares Jesus to be the Son of God, speaking, teaching, and acting as the channel for God's infinite wisdom. And Mohammed, the founder of Islam, has been worshipped through the centuries by Muslims as the Prophet through whom Allah revealed the Holy Qur'an.

These holy teachers devoted their lives to guiding humanity toward paths of goodness. They gave messages suited to the vital necessities of their times; but the inner truths of their teachings have not become less relevant today.

# All Religions Inspired by God

The Lord said to Moses, "Come up to me on the mountain, and wait there; and I will give you the tables of stone, with the law and the commandment, which I have written."

*Judaism*

The words that I speak unto you I speak not of myself: but the Father that dwelleth in me, he doeth the works.

*Christianity*

The Qur'an through the Prophet's lips did come, But whosoever says God spoke it not, speaks false.

*Islam*

I God have given this knowledge to mankind from age
to age.

God sent me into this world with the following orders . . .
"Go and spread My religion there,
And restrain the world from senseless acts."

*Sikhism*

The One Life of all life now lives in me!
Then Truth, God, came and dwelt within my heart,
And was my understanding, ear, eye, speech.

*Sufism*

# God Is Love

This saying expresses what humanity perceives as the concentrated essence of God. Love is the sum total of all other conceptions we have of the Divine—forgiving, wise, compassionate, infinitely creative, eternal, and extremely personal to each individual.

In the Sanskrit language, the universality of God is expressed in the term *Sat-Chit-Ananda*. *Sat* can be translated as "existence"—showing that God is eternal and infinite. *Chit* means "intelligent"—expressing the creative and omniscient aspects of God. *Ananda* is often translated as "bliss" or "joy"— implying that God is radiant with happiness, peace, and love. The aspect of love is most dear to humanity, which cherishes the very thought of love from youth to old age.

We feel that we are all the children of God, and we feel secure in the knowledge that the love of God is infused into even the smallest aspect of human life.

The wise of every generation have declared that they have drawn their wisdom from a universal source, and that this source is filled with unbounded truth, love, and joy. When fully understood, the conviction that God is love will unite people everywhere.

# God Is Love

God is love, and he who abides in love abides in God, and God abides in him.

*Christianity*

As the radiant sun shines upon all regions above, below, and across, so does this glorious one God of love protect and guide all creatures.

*Buddhism*

The Supreme loves and nourishes all things.

*Taoism*

All beside love is but words.

*Bahá'í*

It makes no difference as to the name of God,
since love is the real God of all the world.

*Apache*
*Native American*


Sane and insane, all are searching lovelorn
For Him, in mosque, temple, church, alike.
For only God is the One God of Love,
And Love calls from all these, each one
       His home.

*Sufism*

# Man Is Made
# in the Image of God

What do the scriptures mean when they say that "man is made in the image of God"? Perhaps that man has been created with infinite complexity and potential. Or that we, among all living things, have free will to choose our paths in life. We can rise to encompass the highest thoughts of angels, or degrade ourselves to the unfeeling level of beasts.

Perhaps most of all, this saying indicates that we have the ability to objectively witness and evaluate our own actions. We can judge what we and others have done. We can administer justice. We can learn, change, and grow. We can teach our children, and we can record our best thoughts and intentions in writings that will influence future generations long after we have passed on. These are godlike activities when compared with the capacities of all other creatures.

God has given man everything needed to reflect His own nature—intelligence, creativity, and the unique sense of self-awareness. When we use these qualities to understand and base our actions on the truths shared by all religions, we can begin to appreciate the Divine within ourselves, and we can lead our lives in such a way that we radiate this understanding to others around us.

# Man Is Made
# in the Image of God

God created man in His own image, in the image of God created He him.

*Judaism*

On God's own nature has been molded man's.

*Islam*

O man, in God's image is he.

*Sikhism*

The Supreme gives man His expression, and gives him
His form.

*Taoism*

Know ye not that ye are the temple of God, and that the
Spirit of God dwelleth in you?

*Christianity*

I created thee, have engraven on thee Mine image, and
revealed to thee My beauty.

*Bahá'í*

# Living in Unity

It has been one of the world's great ongoing challenges that the holy sites of Christianity, Judaism, and Islam are located in the same region of the world. Similarly, many of the sacred locations of the Hindu and Islamic religions are shared in India and other nations. Questions of possession and ownership surrounding these sites have led to some of history's most tragic conflicts.

Sacred sites and places of pilgrimage give a tangible expression to the sources of one's religion, and keep the mind appreciative of higher spiritual ideals. Religious sites are charged from time immemorial with the spiritual energy of holy beings, and are revered as locations consecrated by God. It will be a blessed day, undoubtedly pleasing to God, when we have resolved our quarrels, and the intrinsic holiness of these spiritual sites is shared by all.

How can centuries of hatred be turned to love? There is only one way: by appreciating the underlying unity of all people, and by basing all our interactions on this eternal truth.

We are all inseparably linked, and our destinies are forever intertwined. Gradually, we are learning that our own happiness depends on the happiness of others—among nations, cultures, and religions, just as among members of an individual family. This tendency will not cease, because unity by its very nature is more powerful than diversity.

# Living in Unity

The soul of Oneness is the soul of man,
The soul of all-inclusive Sympathy,
Of Unity and of non-separateness.

*Sufism*

The well-being of mankind, its peace and security, are
unattainable unless and until its unity is firmly established.

*Bahá'í*

Blessed is the teaching of truth,
Blessed the harmony of the community,
Blessed the union of those who live in peace

*Buddhism*

Behold, how good and pleasant it is when brothers dwell in unity!

*Judaism*

There can never be peace between nations until it is first known that true peace is within the souls of men.

*Oglala Sioux*
*Native American*

Common be your intentions; common be the wishes of your hearts; common be your thoughts, so that there may be thorough union among you.

*Hinduism*

# All Created Things Pass Away; Only the Inner Spirit Remains

Time exposes life's superficial aspects; only fundamental truths endure. When looking at ancient buildings and at monuments constructed thousands of years ago, we see that decorations and ornaments have vanished. Even walls and roofs have crumbled. Only foundations and central pillars remain. Similarly, the limbs and extremities of ancient statues often have fallen away, leaving only those portions supported by strong central structures.

The same is true in our lives. The ever-changing outer world gradually teaches us to look for and appreciate inner, more lasting values. Ultimately we are led to the realization that only our inner spirit remains untouched by change. The innermost nature of our being remains steadfast through all passing joys and pains.

It is at the core of our being that our lives touch the Eternal, and it is from here that we derive our true strength.

# All Created Things Pass Away;
# Only the Inner Spirit Remains

The world passeth away . . . but he that doeth the will of
God abideth for ever.

*Christianity*

Everything that you have shall pass away, but that which is
with Allah is Eternal.

*Islam*

God is our refuge and strength, a very present help in
trouble. Therefore will not we fear, though the earth be
removed, and though the mountains be carried into the
midst of the sea.

*Judaism*

# All Created Things Pass Away;
# Only the Inner Spirit Remains

Deep within abides another life, not like the life of the senses, escaping sight, unchanging. This endures when all created things have passed away.

*Hinduism*

By wisdom, by inner awareness and restraint, one may create for oneself an island no flood can overwhelm.

*Buddhism*

# The Blessing of Prayer

Oil streaming rapidly through a narrow pipeline inevitably becomes turbulent and agitated. To alleviate this turbulence—which can damage the entire pipeline—engineers design the tubing so that its diameter widens at intervals. This allows the oil to spread out, to slow down and flow more evenly, so that when the tubing again narrows and the oil speeds up, the stream is smooth and free-flowing.

Our lives in many ways are similar. The frenzy, stress, turmoil, and anxiety of the world could prove too much if we did not take moments of inner calm. This allows us to refocus, to rejuvenate our souls, and to reinvigorate our daily lives.

Prayer, in particular, is our connection with the Divine. It allows us to directly communicate our needs and feelings with a Higher Power, which—as every religion clearly states—listens to all we say and is responsive to our needs.

# The Blessing of Prayer

When the world is in distress, it heartily prays. The True
One attentively listens and with His kind disposition grants
consolation.

*Sikhism*


Whatsoever ye shall ask in prayer, believing, ye shall receive.

*Christianity*


And the Lord says, "Pray unto Me, I will answer your
prayer."

*Islam*


The Lord is nigh unto all them that call upon Him, to all
that call upon Him in truth.

*Judaism*

One should delight in prayer to God. If you make this your foundation, the past will not tarnish you.

*Hinduism*

Prayer is of the foremost importance in appealing for the divine grace, and uprightness is a fundamental quality if one would obtain the unseen protection.

*Shintoism*

# The Peace That Passes
# All Understanding

Saint Thomas Aquinas is the author of a number of the world's most enlightened spiritual writings. His great book *Summa Theologica* is one of the pillars of the Catholic faith, though written more than seven hundred years ago.

Near the end of his life, when he had not written for some time, he was asked if he would continue his work. He replied, "All that I have written now appears to me of no greater value than mere straw."

Saint Thomas had experienced a revelation, one so profound and intensely personal that he could not express it in words. It eclipsed all that he had previously written about logic and reason as means to understand God, and it led him to an inner peace and joy that was beyond understanding, beyond description.

Just so, Jesus remained silent when asked by Pilate, "What is Truth?" Christ understood that the peace of God could not be expressed in words. Similarly, the enlightened sages of

Hinduism, Sikhism, Sufism, and other great religions experienced within themselves a peace that passed all understanding, and defied expression.

Our connection with the Divine is beyond words and thought. "Be still, and know that I am God," says the Old Testament of the Holy Bible. Only in silent union can we truly understand the Divine. In the highest sense, contact with the Divine is a state of awareness that transcends understanding. It brings a peace that cannot be described, only experienced.

# The Peace That Passes
# All Understanding

The peace of God, which passes all understanding, will keep your hearts and your minds in Christ Jesus.

*Christianity*

His mind becomes calm. His word and deed are calm. Such is the state of tranquillity of one who has attained Nirvana through the realization of truth.

*Buddhism*

He who has inner joy, who has inner gladness, has found the inner Light. He has become one with infinite peace.

*Hinduism*

For them will be a Home of Peace with their Lord: He will be their Friend, because they practiced righteousness.

*Islam*


The Lord bless thee, and keep thee: The Lord make his face shine upon thee, and be gracious unto thee: The Lord lift up his countenance to thee, and give thee peace.

*Judaism*


Those whose hearts are in a state of calmness give forth a divine radiance by which they know truth.

*Taoism*

# Thy Will Be Done

The scriptures of the world's religions declare that each human being is essentially an unbounded and immortal soul. Each individual is an expression of the Divine, and every person has the potential to become aware of the Divine within.

For this reason, to pray "Thy will be done" does not imply that we wish some outer, all-powerful force to predominate, overriding our "erroneous" or "evil" desires. Instead, the essence of this prayer expresses our wish that the innermost, purest, highest ideals of our own being will rise up to inspire and guide all our thoughts and actions. The prayer *Thy will be done* is an expression of the highest aspiration of religious thought, showing our longing to live and act in harmony with our Creator.

# Thy Will Be Done

Thy will be done, On earth as it is in heaven.

*Christianity*

My doubts are no more, my faith is firm; and now I can say: "Thy will be done."

*Hinduism*

I delight to do thy will, O my God: yea, thy law is within my heart.

*Judaism*

It is God who doeth whatever is done.

*Sikhism*

# Thy Will Be Done

Who has a better religion than he who resigneth himself to God?

*Islam*

Always strive to accord with the will of heaven,
so shall you be seeking for much happiness.

*Confucianism*

# Prayers of the Religions

The prayers of the world's religions have a common theme: the desire and need to make contact with God, and through the Almighty Power to be shown the path on earth that leads to freedom, health, prosperity, and knowledge. These are the things that every person wants. These aspirations are the goals of life.

The central prayers of the religions ask for guidance in achieving these aspirations. Their common goal shows the essential Oneness of the human spirit.

# Prayers of the Religions

Our Father who art in heaven, Hallowed be thy name. Thy kingdom come, Thy will be done, On earth as it is in heaven. Give us this day our daily bread; And forgive us our debts, As we also have forgiven our debtors; And lead us not into temptation, But deliver us from evil. Amen.

*Christianity*

Unto thee, O Lord, do I lift up my soul. O my God, I trust in thee: let me not be ashamed, let not mine enemies triumph over me . . . Show me thy ways, O Lord; teach me thy paths. Lead me in thy truth, and teach me: for thou art the God of my salvation.

*Judaism*

Praise be to Allah, the Lord of all creatures; the most merciful, the king of the Day of Judgment. Thee do we worship, and of Thee do we beg assistance. Direct us in the right way, in the way of those to whom Thou has been gracious; not of those against whom Thou art incensed, nor of those who go astray.

*Islam*

Supreme Lord! From the unreal lead me to the real!
From darkness lead me to light!
From death lead me to immortality! Aum.

*Hinduism*

May all beings everywhere plagued with sufferings of body and mind, obtain an ocean of happiness and joy.

# Prayers of the Religions

May those feeble with cold find warmth,

And may those oppressed with heat be cooled.

May the naked find clothing, the hungry food.

May all who are ill quickly be freed from illness.

May no living creature ever suffer, commit evil or fall ill.

May those who find themselves in trackless, fearful

wildernesses, the children, the aged, the unprotected,

be guarded by beneficent celestials,

And may they swiftly attain Buddhahood.

*Buddhism*

Grant me this boon that I may never turn

From the Right Path of Duty; never fear

To war against evil; and may always win!

I fold my hands in humble prayer to Thee!

I bend my head in lowly reverence!

Ordain that Thy Path may be trod by all!

Give me the strength to make it plain to men!

*Sikhism*

# Aum! Amīn! Amēn! Amen!

# ANNOTATIONS

ABBREVIATIONS AND MAIN SOURCES—Christianity: all references from the New Testament of the Holy Bible, King James Version (KJV) or Revised Standard Version (RSV). Judaism: Old Testament of the Holy Bible, KJV and RSV; Talmud. Islam: The Holy Qur'an (Qur'an); Hadith. Buddhism: Dhammapada (Dham.). Hinduism: Bhagavad Gita; Mahabharata (Maha.); Hitopadesa (Hi.). Confucianism: Analects of Confucius (Analects); Mencius. Bahá'í: selected quotes. Sikhism: quoted Guru (selected quotes with volume and page number in M.A. Macauliffe). Taoism: Tao Teh Ching (TTC). Sufism: selected writings. Native American: all from Zona. Jainism: noted scriptures. Shintoism: noted scriptures. African wisdom: from Mbiti and other sources. References also to page numbers in *Essential Unity of All Religions (EU)*, *Readings from World Religions (WR)*, and *Wisdom of the Living Religions (LR)*.

THE GOLDEN RULE: Christianity, accepted common version (also Matthew 7:12, Luke 6:31); Judaism, Talmud, Rabbi Hillel (also in Moed, Shabbath); Islam, Mishkat-el-Masabih; Buddhism, Udanavarga 5.8; Confucianism, Analects 15:23; Hinduism, Maha., Anusasana Parva (Book 13) CXIII; Sikhism, Guru Angad, vol. 2, 29; Jainism, Sutrakritanga Sutra 1.11.33; Taoism, Tai-Shang Kan-Ying Pien; Bahá'í, Bahá'u'lláh.

Love Thy Neighbor: Judaism, Leviticus 19:18 KJV; Christianity, John 13:34–35 RSV; Hinduism, Maha., Anusasana Parva (Book 13) CXIII; Buddhism, Dham., *WR* 174; Confucianism, Shu King 5.17.2; Islam, Hadith.

The World Is Our Family: Christianity, Acts 17:26 KJV; Hinduism, Bhavishya Purana III, IV, Chapter 23; Judaism, Malachi 2:10 KJV; Islam, Hadith; Shintoism, Oracle of the Deity of Atsuta; Native American, Zona.

There Is One God: Christianity, Ephesians 4:6 KJV; Judaism, Deuteronomy 4:39 RSV; Hinduism, Svetasvatara Upanishad 6.11; Sikhism, The Japji, vol. 1, 195; Sufism, Sufi writings; Bahá'í, Bahá'ulláh.

More Blessed to Give Than to Receive: Christianity, Acts 20:35 KJV; Taoism, TTC 81:2; Sikhism, Asa Ki War Sloka 6; Islam, Qur'an 57:18; Hinduism, Maha. 12.293.3; Judaism, Psalms 41:1 KJV.

Do Not Harm Anything: Hinduism, Manu 2:161; Buddhism, Dham. 185; Christianity, Ephesians 4:32 KJV; Jainism, Sutrakritanga 1.11.12; Judaism, Zechariah 7:9 RSV; Islam, Hadith.

Preserve the Earth: Christianity, Hebrews 6:7 KJV; Buddhism, Sayings of the Buddha; Islam, Hadith; Native American, Zona; Hinduism, Vedas, various sources; Confucianism, Mencius 1.1.3.3.

Heaven Is Within: Christianity, Luke 17:20–21 KJV; Confucianism, Analects 15:20; Buddhism, *Major Writings of Nichiren Daishonin*, vol. 1, "On Attaining Buddahood," 3–5; Sufism, Sufi Writings; Hinduism, Katha Upanishad 2; Sikhism, Guru Nanak, vol. 1, 330.

As Ye Sow, So Shall Ye Reap: Buddhism, Ta-chwang-Yan-King-Lun Sermon 57; Christianity, Galatians 6:7 RSV; Sikhism, Guru Nanak 1, 11;

Judaism, Proverbs 11:25 RSV; Confucianism, Mencius 1.2.12.2; Hinduism, Manu 9.40.

CONQUER WITH LOVE: Islam, Qur'an 41:38; Christianity, Romans 12:21 KJV; Hinduism, Maha., Anusasana Parva (Book 13) CXIII; Judaism, Proverbs 15:1 RSV; Buddhism, Fo-Sho-Hing-Tsan-King; Native American, Zona.

BLESSED ARE THE PEACEMAKERS: Christianity, Matthew 5:9 KJV; Islam, Hadith; Hinduism, Kiratarjuniya of Bharavi; Judaism, Proverbs 12:20 KJV; Bahá'í, 'Abdu'l-Bahá, Paris Talks, October 21, 1911; Buddhism, Cula-Hatthi-Padapama Sutta.

TRUTH IS UNIVERSAL: Christianity, II Timothy 3:16–17 RSV; Islam, Qur'an 3:84; Buddhism, Ashoka's Edicts, Rock Edicts 1.2; Hinduism, Shrimad Bhagavatam 4.4.19; Confucianism, Chung Yung 13.1; Sufism, Prayers of Hazrat-o-Murshid.

BETTER TO EXAMINE THE SELF: Confucianism, Mencius 4.1–2; Christianity, Matthew 7:5 RSV; Buddhism, Dham. 252; Hinduism, Garuda Purana 113.57, Taoism, TTC 33:11; Sikhism, Guru Amar Das, vol. 2, 167.

HONOR THY FATHER AND MOTHER: Judaism, Proverbs 6:20 RSV; Christianity, Matthew 15:4 KJV; Hinduism, Avaiyar, WR 17; Islam, Hadith; Buddhism, Sutta-Nipata 261; Confucianism, Mencius 4.1.11.

JUDGE NOT: Christianity, Matthew 7:1 KJV; Judaism, Talmud, Nezekin, Pirke Aboth; Buddhism, Siamese Buddhist Proverb; Islam, Qur'an 10:109; Bahá'í, 'Abdu'l-Bahá, Paris Talks, Part II, November 13, 1911.

Love Your Enemies: Christianity, Luke 6:27–28 KJV; Islam, Hadith; Confucianism, Analects 14:36; Judaism, Proverbs 25:2 KJV; Hinduism, Maha., Vana Parva (Book 3); Jainism, Dasha-Vaikalika Sutra 8.39.

Wisdom Is More Precious Than Riches: Islam, Hadith; Christianity, Matthew 6:19 KJV; Judaism, Proverbs 16:16 KJV; Buddhism, Nidhikanda Sutta of the Khuddakanaikaya; Hinduism, Garuda Purana 115.

Man Does Not Live by Bread Alone: Christianity, Luke 4:4 KJV; Hinduism, Katha Upanishad 1; Sikhism, The Japji, vol. 1, 213; Judaism, Deuteronomy 8:3 KJV; Confucianism, Analects 15:31.

Blessed to Forgive: Judaism, Rokeach, *WR* 56; Christianity, Matthew 18:21–22 RSV; Islam, Qur'an 42:40; Sikhism, Kabir, vol. 6, 302; Taoism, TTC 63; Buddhism, Dham. 5.

Speak Truth: Christianity, Ephesians 4:25 KJV; Judaism, Zechariah 8:16 KJV; Buddhism, Dham. 408; Islam, Qur'an 2:39; Hinduism, Taittiriyaka Upanishad 1.10; African wisdom, Ashanti proverb; Confucianism, Mencius 4.1.12.2–3.

We Are Known by Our Deeds, Not by Our Religion: Sikhism, Adi Granth, vol. 2, 162; Christianity, Romans 2:6 KJV; Judaism, Talmud, Nezekin, Pirke Aboth; Native American, Zona; Buddhism, Sutta Nipata 1.7.

Be Slow to Anger: Judaism, Proverbs 14:29 RSV; Hinduism, Bhagavad Gita 2:56; Christianity, Ephesians 4:26 KJV; Islam, Hadith; Shintoism, Sayings from the Chronicles of Japan; Buddhism, Dham. 222.

Follow the Spirit of the Scriptures, Not the Letter: Christianity, II Corinthians 3:6 KJV; Judaism, Yevamos 79a; Islam, Hadith; Buddhism, Tevigga Sutta 1:46; Hinduism, Upanishads, *EU* 542; Sufism, Sufi writings.

START WHEN YOUNG TO SEEK WISDOM: Judaism, Apocrypha, Ecclesiasticus; Hinduism, Avaiyar, WR 17; Christianity, Matthew 6:33 KJV; Islam, Hadith; Buddhism, Dham. 382.

HONOR THE ELDERLY: Buddhism, Dham. 109; Judaism, Job 12:12 KJV; Confucianism, Mencius, 1.1.7.12; Christianity, I Timothy 5:1 RSV; Native American, Zona; Islam, Hadith; African wisdom, Nilotic proverb.

KEEP COMPANY WITH THE WISE: Judaism, Proverbs 13:20 RSV; Hinduism, Maha. 5.36.13; Islam, Hadith; Buddhism, Dham. 208; Confucianism, Analects 4:17; Sikhism, Guru Ram Das, vol. 2, 346.

THERE ARE MANY PATHS TO GOD: Sufi, Sufi writings; Hinduism, Bhagavad Gita 4:11; Christianity, Romans 8:14 KJV; Confucianism, I Ching, Appended Phrases 2.5; Native American, Zona.

SEEK AND YE SHALL FIND: Christianity, Matthew 7:7 KJV; Judaism, Deuteronomy 4:29 KJV; Hinduism, Bhagavad Gita 6:44; Sikhism, Guru Arjan, vol. 3, 229; Buddhism, Dham. 121; Islam, Hadith.

BETTER TO RULE THE SPIRIT: Christianity, Matthew 16:25–26 KJV; Judaism, Proverbs 16:32 RSV; Buddhism, Dham. 103; Islam, Hadith; Taoism, TTC 33.2; Jainism, Uttaradhyayana Sutra 9.36.

GOD IS FORGIVING: Judaism, 2 Chronicles 30:9 KJV; Islam, Hadith; Christianity, I John 1:9 KJV; Hinduism, Bhagavad Gita 9:30–31; Taoism, T'ao Shang Kan Ying P'ien 1200–1230; Sikhism, Kabir's Slokas 155.

BE LOVING, AS GOD IS LOVING TO ALL: Buddhism, The Ninth Perfection, Sutta-Pitaka, Buddha-Vasama; Christianity, Matthew 5:45 KJV; Judaism, Talmud, Moed-Taanith; Hinduism, Maha., Shanti Parva (Book 12) LXXIII; Taoism, TTC 8; Native American, Zona; Islam, Hadith.

MODERATION IN ALL THINGS: Taoism, TTC 59; Confucianism, Shi King 3.3.2.8.5–6; Hinduism, Bhagavad Gita 6:16–17; Christianity, Philippians 4:5 KJV; Shintoism, Inazo Nitobe; Islam, Hadith.

PRIDE GOES BEFORE A FALL: Judaism, Proverbs 16:18 RSV; Confucianism, Shu King 2.2.3; Hinduism, Shatapatha Brahmana, *EU* 359; Christianity, I Peter 5:5 KJV; Islam, Qur'an 16:24; Taoism, TTC 39.

THE SOUL IS ETERNAL: Jainism, Sutrakritanga, 1.1.1.16; Christianity, Galatians 6:8 KJV; Judaism, Psalms 23:6 KJV; Bahá'í, Bahá'u'lláh; Hinduism, Bhagavad Gita 11:4; Islam, Hadith.

IN THE BEGINNING: Sikhism, Guru Nanak, vol. 1, 165; Hinduism, Rig Veda 10.11.1.1–2; Judaism, Genesis 1:1–3 KJV; Christianity, John 1:1–3 KJV; Taoism, TTC 25; Islam, Qur'an 57:4–5.

GOD CREATED ALL THINGS: Christianity, Hebrews 3:4, RSV; Hinduism, Vishnu Purana 1.1.35; Confucianism, Li Chi 9.2.8; Judaism, Jeremiah 10:12, RSV; Islam, Qur'an 6:1; Sikhism, The Japji, vol. 1, 212; African wisdom, Mbiti.

GOD IS BEYOND COMPREHENSION: Judaism, Job 37:5 RSV; Christianity, Romans 11:33 KJV; Sufism, Sufi writings; Taoism, TTC 4; Islam, Qur'an 31:27; Sikhism, Guru Arjan, vol. 3, 323.

BE CONTENT: Christianity, Matthew 6:25–26 RSV; Sikhism, The Rahiras, Guru Arjan, vol. 1, 254; Buddhism, Dham. 204; Judaism, Proverbs 14:30 RSV; Hinduism, Manu 4.12; Shintoism, God of Fujiyama.

SEEK THE GOOD OF THE WORLD: Hinduism, proverb; Confucianism, Analects 7:27; Taoism, TTC 28; Shintoism, Shinto prayer; Christianity, Philippians 4:8 KJV.

SPEAK GENTLY: Buddhism, Dham. 133; Christianity, Colossians 4:6 RSV; Sikhism, Bhagats of the Granth Sahib, Shaikh Farid CXXIX, vol. 6, 414; African wisdom, Nilotic proverb; Hinduism, Bhagavad Gita 7:15; Islam, Qur'an 31:17; Native American, Zona; Judaism, Proverbs 25:11 RSV.

DO NOT LOOK FOR FAULTS IN OTHERS: Confucianism, Mencius 7.2.32.3; Islam, Instructions of Ali Ibn-abi Talib, WR 285; Shintoism, Precepts of Jyegasu; Christianity, Romans 2:1 KJV; Bahá'í, Bahá'ulláh; Buddhism, Dham. 253; Taoism, Kwang-Tze EU 542.

THE BLESSING OF CHARITY: Christianity, Matthew 5:42 KJV; Islam, Hadith; Judaism, Proverbs 19:17 KJV; Buddhism, The First Perfection, Sutta-Pitaka, Buddha Vasma; Hinduism, Rig Veda 10.10.5.3; Confucianism, Mencius 2.1.7.2.

THE BLESSING OF HOSPITALITY: Judaism, Exodus 22:21 KJV; Hinduism, Maha., Anusasana Parva, VII; Islam, Masnavi, WR 281; Christianity, Hebrews 13:1–2 KJV; Shintoism, Kurozumi Kyo/Konko Kyo.

GIVE WITHOUT THOUGHT OF REWARD: Hinduism, Bhagavad Gita 17:20; Islam, Qur'an 2:273; Christianity, Matthew 6:1 KJV; Judaism, Talmud, Nezekin, Baba Bathra; Taoism, T'ao Shang Kan Ying P'ien, WR 111.

GIVE AND YOU SHALL RECEIVE AGAIN: Christianity, Luke 6:38 KJV; Judaism, Ecclesiastes 11:1 RSV; Islam, Qur'an 57:18; Taoism, TTC 36; Hinduism, Hi., LR 142; Confucianism, Mencius 1.2.12.

THE GOODNESS OF WEALTH: Judaism, Proberbs 15:6 KJV; Islam, Hadith; Jainism, Uttaradhyayana-Sutra, 13.10; Buddhism, Sutta-Nipata; Confucianism, Lun Yu 7:15; Hinduism, Garuda Purana 115.12.

KNOWLEDGE IS THE BASIS FOR SUCCESS: Christianity, I Corinthians 14:10 KJV; Buddhism, Jatakas; Judaism, Proverbs 24:3–4 RSV; Confucianism, Analects 1:2; Islam, Hadith.

PERSEVERENCE IS THE KEY TO SUCCESS: Buddhism, Sutta-Pitaka; Judaism, Proverbs 21:5 RSV; Confucianism, Analects 13:17; Shintoism, Precepts of Jyegasu; Islam, Masnavi, WR 261; Taoism, TTC 64.

WE CREATE OUR OWN DESTINY: Christianity, Matthew 16:27 KJV; Buddhism, Dham. 165; Judaism, Psalms 62:12 KJV; Confucianism, Mencius 2.1.4.5; Islam, Qur'an 99:7–8; Hinduism, Garuda Purana 113.29.

THE LOVE OF GOOD WORKS: Buddhism, Dham. 16; Hinduism, Manu 4.175; Christianity, Matthew 5:6 KJV; Confucianism, Analects 6:18; Islam, Hadith; Judaism, Psalms 1:2 KJV.

GOD IS FOUND IN THE HEART: Shintoism, Revelation to Mikado Seiwa; Sikhism, Guru Nanak, vol. 1, 330; Christianity, I Corinthians 3:16 KJV; Hinduism, Bhagavad Gita 13:17; Islam, Khalifa Ali; Jainism, Samayika-Patha.

MAN PROPOSES, GOD DISPOSES: Islam, Hadith; Sikhism, Arjan's Sukhmani, Ashtapadi 14, WR 296; Christianity, I Corinthians 3:6 KJV; Hinduism, Hi.; African Wisdom, Mbiti; Judaism, Proverbs 16:9 KJV.

HE WHO SLAYS ANYONE: Judaism, Talmud, Nezekin, Sanhedrin; Islam, Qur'an 5:32; Christianity, Matthew 26:52 KJV; Buddhism, Dham. 130; Jainism, Sutrakritanga 1.1.4.2.

AVOID DOING WHAT YOU KNOW TO BE WRONG: Judaism, Talmud, Pirke Aboth; Islam, Hadith; Jainism, Sutrakritanga 1.2.3.15; Christianity, James 4:17 RSV: Hinduism, Bhagavad Gita 2:9; Confucianism, Mencius 7.1.17.

DEFINITIONS OF RELIGION: Buddhism, Ashoka's Edicts, The Seven Pillar Edicts 2; Christianity, Galatians 5:14 KJV; Hinduism, Hi.; Bahá'í, WR 263–64; Taoism, T'ao Shang Kan Ying P'ien; Islam, Hadith.

ALL RELIGIONS INSPIRED BY GOD: Judaism, Exodus 24:12 RSV; Christianity, John 14:10 KJV; Islam, EU 341; Hinduism, Upanishads; Sikhism, Guru Gobind Sing, vol. 5, 299.

GOD IS LOVE: Christianity, I John 4:16 RSV; Hinduism, Svetasvatara Upanishad 5.4; Taoism, TTC 34.2; Bahá'í, Bahá'í sayings; Native American, Zona; Sufism, Sufi writings.

MAN IS MADE IN THE IMAGE OF GOD: Judaism, Genesis 1:27 KJV; Islam, Hadith; Sikhism, Teg Bahadur, vol. 4, 415; Taoism, Kwang Tze 5.5; Christianity, I Corinthians 3:16 KJV; Bahá'í, Bahá'u'lláh.

LIVING IN UNITY: Sufism, Sufi writings; Bahá'í, Bahá'u'lláh; Buddhism, Dham. 194; Judaism, Psalms 133:1 RSV; Native American, Zona; Hinduism, Rig Veda 10.12.40.4.

ALL CREATED THINGS PASS AWAY; ONLY THE INNER SPIRIT REMAINS: Christianity, I John 2:17 KJV; Islam, Qur'an 16:97; Judaism, Psalms 46:1–2 KJV; Hinduism, Bhagavad Gita 8:20; Buddhism, Dham. 25; Sufism, Sufi writings.

THE BLESSINGS OF PRAYER: Sikhism, Guru Amar Das, vol. 1, 41; Christianity, Matthew 21:22 KJV; Islam, Qur'an 40:61; Judaism, Psalms 145:18 KJV; Hinduism, Svetasvatara Upanishad 2.3; Shintoism, Shinto Gobusho.

THE PEACE THAT PASSES ALL UNDERSTANDING: Christianity, Philippians 4:7 RSV; Buddhism, Dham. 96; Hinduism, Bhagavad Gita 5:24; Islam, Qur'an 6:127; Judaism, Numbers 6:24–26; Taoism, Kwang Tze 23.7.

THY WILL BE DONE: Christianity, Matthew 6:10 RSV; Hinduism, Bhagavad Gita 18:73; Judaism, Psalms 40:8 KJV; Sikhism, Guru Amar Das, vol. 1, L (in Macauliffe Introduction); Islam, Qur'an 4:124; Confucianism, Mencius 2.1.4.6.

PRAYERS OF THE RELIGIONS: Christianity, Matthew 6:9–13 (the Lord's Prayer) RSV; Judaism, Psalms 25:1, 2, 4, 5 KJV; Islam, Qur'an 1:1–7 (Al-Fatiha); Hinduism, Brihad-Aranyaka Upanishad 1.3.28; Buddhism, Bodhicharyavatara of Shantideva; Sikhism, Guru Govinda Sinha.

# CHRONOLOGY

The written Vedic Texts of Hinduism
(oral tradition dates from ancient India) ............................c. 4500–3000 B.Ç.

Cultural wisdom of all continents—
African, European, North and South American, Asian
(oral traditions dating from prehistory) ...............................c. 4000–3000 B.C.

Krishna, Hindu Deity ..........................................................c. 1500 B.C.

Shinto texts (oral tradition dates
from prehistoric Japan) ........................................................c. 1500 B.C.

Judaism ..................................................................................c. 1300 B.C.

Moses .....................................................................................c. 1300 B.C.

King Solomon .......................................................................c. 970 B.C.

Lao Tse, principal founder of Taoism ...................................c. 604–515 B.C.

Mahavira, principal founder of Jainism ...............................599–527 B.C.

Buddha ..................................................................................c. 573–483 B.C.

Confucius ...............................................................................551–479 B.C.

Socrates ........................................................................ c. 470–399 B.C.

Plato ............................................................................... 429–348 B.C.

Mencius, Chinese contributor to Confucianism .............. c. 370–290 B.C.

Jesus .............................................................................. 5 B.C.–A.D. 30

Paul ............................................................................... A.D. 3–66

The *Codex Sinaiticus*,
earliest copy of the Bible in Greek ................................ c. A.D. 350

Mohammed ................................................................... A.D. 570–632

Sufism ........................................................................... c. A.D. 800

Guru Nanak, founder of Sikhism .................................. A.D. 1469–1538

Bahá'ulláh, founder of Bahá'í ....................................... A.D. 1817–1892

# SOURCES AND
# SUGGESTED READINGS

Many of the following books contain excellent descriptions of the world's great religions, as well as complete or partial translations of their central scriptures. Almost all these books can be found in large libraries or obtained through interlibrary loan services. With the exceptions of the Holy Bible and the Holy Qur'an, only a few can be found in bookstores—although many are available through their respective religious organizations and on the Internet.

When comparing translations of specific scriptural passages by various translators, significant differences often can be found. In some instances, the wording is so different that it's difficult to recognize the passage, even when the exact location within the scripture is known.

The sayings used in *Oneness* were selected based on what I felt were their appropriateness of wording and style. They capture the original intent, and express both the "letter" and the "spirit" of the precept.

Al-Suhrawdy, Allama Sir Abdullah. *The Wisdom of the East Series: The Sayings of Mohammed.* London: John Murray, 1941.

Champion, Selwyn Gurney, and Dorothy Short. *Readings from World Religions*. Boston: The Beacon Press, 1951.

Cowell, E. B. *Jatakas*. London: Cambridge University Press, 1895.

Dhammika, Ven S. *The Edicts of King Ashoka*. Buddhist Publication Society, 1993. DhamaNet Edition, 1994.

Das, Bhagavan. *The Essential Unity of All Religions*. Wheaton, Ill.: Theosophical Press, 1939.

Gaer, Joseph. *The Wisdom of the Living Religions*. New York: Dodd, Mead & Company, 1956.

Ganguli, Kisari Mohan. *The Mahabharata*. Volumes 1–12. New Delhi, India: Munshiram Manoharlal Publishers Pvt. Ltd., 1970.

*Gleanings from the Writings of Bahá'u'lláh*. Trans. Shoghi Effendi. Second rev. ed. Wilmette, Ill.: Bahá'í Publishing Trust, 1976.

The Holy Bible. King James Version.

The Holy Bible. Revised Standard Version.

Hume, E. H. *Treasure-House of the Living Religions*. New York, London: Charles Scribner's Sons, 1933.

Johnson, Francis. *Hitopadesa: The Book of Wholesome Counsel*. Rev. Lionel D. Barnett, London: Chapman and Hall, 1923.

The Koran (Qur'an). Trans. George Sale. Philadelphia: J. B. Lippincott & Co., 1864.

Legge, James, D.D., L.L.D. *The Life and Works of Mencius*. London: Trübner and Co., 1875.

Macauliffe, Max Arthur. *The Sikh Religion: Its Gurus, Sacred Writings and Authors*. Volumes 1–6. Bombay, India: Oxford University Press, 1963.

Mbiti, John S. *Introduction to African Religion*. Oxford: Heinemann Educational Publishers, 1991.

Old, W. G. *Shu King*. New York: Theosophical Publishing Society, London & Benares, 1904.

Oriental Literature: The Literature of China (including the Analects of Confucius). Rev. ed. New York: Colonial Press, 1900.

*The Sacred Books of China: The Texts of Taoism*. Trans. James Legge, D.D., L.L.D. London: Oxford University Press, 1891.

*Sacred Books of the East* (including the Vedic Hymns and the Dhammapada of Buddhism). Rev. ed. New York: P. F. Collier & Sons, 1900.

*Sacred Books of the East: Laws of Manu*. Trans. George Bühler. Oxford: Clarendon Press, 1886.

*Sacred Books of the East. The Upanishads*. Trans. F. Max Müller. Oxford: Clarendon Press, 1879.

Zona, Guy A. *The Soul Would Have No Rainbow If the Eyes Had No Tears, and Other Native American Proverbs*. New York: Touchstone, 1994.

# PERSONAL NOTES

# PERSONAL NOTES

# PERSONAL NOTES

Ruth S. Moses

# ABOUT THE AUTHOR

Jeffrey Moses studied as an undergraduate at UCLA and has an M.A. in the philosophy of education from the University of Colorado at Boulder. He has spent more than twenty years researching the world's greatest scriptures, and has traveled across the country speaking on meditation, stress reduction, and spiritual advancement. Jeffrey lives with his wife, the artist Ruth Moses, on the Emerald Coast of northwest Florida.

Visit the *Oneness* Web site at www.onenessonline.com.